Religion 3
for Young Catholics

Nihil obstat given at Harrisburg, Pennsylvania, on the 25th day of June, 1998, by the Rev. William J. Waltershield, S.T.L., Censor Librorum.

Imprimatur given at Harrisburg, Pennsylvania, on the 25th day of June, 1998, ✝Nicholas C. Dattilo, Bishop of Harrisburg.

The *nihil obstat* and *imprimatur* are official declarations that a book or pamphlet is free of doctrinal or moral error. No implication is contained therein that those who granted the *nihil obstat* or *imprimatur* agree with the contents, opinions, or statements expressed.

by the Seton Staff

The Seton Catholic Family Catechism Series
A Religion Series for Children Educated at Home by their Parents

Seton Press
Front Royal, Virginia

Executive Editor: Dr. Mary Kay Clark
Editors: Seton Staff

© 1998; reprint 2010, 2014, 2017 Seton Home Study School
All rights reserved.
Printed in the United States of America.

Seton Home Study School
1350 Progress Drive
Front Royal, VA 22630
540-636-9990
540-636-1602 fax

For more information, visit us on the Web at www.setonhome.org.
Contact us by e-mail at counselors@setonhome.org.

ISBN: 978-1-60704-045-3

Cover: *The Annunciation*, Edward Burne-Jones

Dedicated to the
Sacred Heart of Jesus

The Annunciation

Contents

First Quarter

God Loves Us

Did you know that God made you because He loves you very much? He made you different from everyone else and He knows everything about you. God wants you to love Him, too! We must love God with our whole hearts. We must love God above all things. God wants us to be happy with Him forever. We pray to God to tell Him we love Him, and to ask Him for His help.

We will learn about God our loving Father Who made us. We will learn about God the Son. He is our dear Jesus. We will learn about God the Holy Spirit. We will learn about Mary, our Blessed Mother. We will learn about God's angels and His saints. We will learn about God's Church, the Catholic Church.

Dear God, show me how to love You
with all my heart.

1. God knows _____ about you.

2. We must love God with our _____ hearts.

3. God wants us to be _____ with Him forever.

God loves each one of us. He loves our parents and our brothers and sisters. He loves us so much that He died for us. He has shown the perfect kind of love. What must we do in return? We must love Him above all things and love our neighbor as ourselves. And who is our neighbor? Does Jesus mean we must be kind to those who live next door to us? Yes, those who live close by are our neighbors, but we have many more neighbors. Our neighbor is anyone we see, talk to, or meet. Our neighbor is the stranger we pass on the street. Our neighbor is every other person in the world.

Our most important neighbors are those in our own family. These are the people with whom Jesus has chosen for us to live and grow up as a family. We must be kind to our friends also. We must respect and obey our parents. Most important, we must love God above all things and all people. Do something extra special for your parents today to show God that you love Him for the family He has given you.

I thank You, dear Jesus, for the loving family You have given me.

1. God loves us so much that He _____ for us.

2. God has shown us the _____ kind of love.

3. We must love God _____ all things.

4. We must love our _____ as ourselves.

Our Lord Jesus is the Son of God the Father. Jesus loves the little children. One day Jesus was very tired. He had been teaching crowds of people all day, so He was resting under a tree. A group of little children wanted to see Him. Christ's close friends, the Apostles, wanted to send the children away because they knew that Jesus needed to rest. Jesus said, "No, let the little children come to Me."

The little children wanted to talk with Jesus. Jesus is always ready to listen to His children. We must talk to Jesus every day. We must pray to Jesus every morning and every night. We talk to Him at home and at Mass. If we are sad, Jesus is ready to comfort us. When we are happy, our dear Jesus is happy, too. Oh, how much He loves us, especially when we talk to Him through our prayers!

Sacred Heart of Jesus,

I believe in Your love for me.

1. Jesus said, "Let the little _____ come to Me."

2. Jesus is always ready to _____.

3. We must _____ to Jesus every day.

God loves us. God does so much for us. What can we do for God? We can pray to Him. God wants us to love Him by giving every little thing we do as a gift to Him. Every morning, we should say our Morning Offering:

O my Jesus,
through the Immaculate Heart of Mary,
I offer You all my prayers, works,
joys, and sufferings of this day.
I offer them for all the intentions
of Your Sacred Heart,
for the salvation of souls,
in reparation for sin,
and for the conversion of all people
to the Holy Catholic Church.
I offer them for the intentions
of our Holy Father the Pope. Amen.

1. Every morning, we should say our

_____ _____.

2. God wants us to _____ Him.

Questions for Week One

(*Questions with an asterisk are taken from the St. Joseph First Communion Catechism.
Prepared from the Official Revised Edition of the Baltimore Catechism, 1963.)

Day 1:

* 1. Did God create all things?

    Yes, God created all things.

* 2. Who made you?

    God made me.

* 3. Why did God make you?

    God made me to show His goodness and to make me happy with Him in Heaven.

Day 2:

1. Does God love us?

    Yes, God loves us.

* 2. What must you do to be happy with God in Heaven?

    To be happy with God in Heaven, I must know Him, love Him, and serve Him in this world.

3. Whom does God command us to love?

    God commands us to love Him with our whole mind, heart, soul, and strength; and love our neighbor as ourselves.

4. Who are the neighbors most important to us?

    The members of our family are our most important "neighbors".

Day 3:

1. Whom does Jesus love in a special way?

    Jesus loves little children in a special way.

2. Who is always ready to listen to us and help us?

    Jesus is always ready to listen to us and help us.

God Is Great

God always was. He was never born. He never had a beginning. God will never have an end. God is eternal. The sun, moon, stars, and planets all had a beginning when God created them. Every person and thing had a beginning.

God is everywhere. No matter where you are or what you are doing, God is there and He sees you. Do you know why you can't see God? God is a spirit and cannot be seen with our human eyes. Although we cannot see God directly, we can see His love in the love that others, such as our parents, show us. God loves us perfectly. We cannot measure His great love, but we can see His love in the many things He created for us, in the many things we see in world around us.

God knows all things. He knows what happened long ago. He knows what will happen tomorrow. He knows about every little and big thing that is happening right now. He knows all our thoughts, words, and actions. He knows everyone's secrets. There is nothing that God does not know.

We can see God's beauty everywhere. All beauty in the world comes from God. All that is beautiful shows us God's beauty. God is more beautiful than anything He has made. There is no one like God. We call God the Supreme Being. This means that there is no one mightier than He.

God can do all things. Did you ever watch a storm at night? Have you ever seen the great streaks of lightning and heard the loud claps of thunder? Have you seen the trees bending and breaking in the strong winds? These things tell you of God's great power. God is greater and more powerful than anyone or anything in this world. Nothing is impossible for God.

Almighty God, have mercy on us!

1. God _____ all things.

2. God _____ was.

3. We call God the _____ _____.

God always was. Before He made us and before He made the angels, there was only God. No one made God; He always was. God will never die. He will live forever.

God never changes. He always remains the same. We call Him the Supreme Being. This means there is no one and nothing higher or mightier than He.

God made everything, so God knows everything. He made us, so He knows everything about us. He knows things we cannot understand. There is nothing anywhere at any time that God does not know. We believe everything God tells us because He is all good, perfectly good, and cannot lie.

God is everywhere, but we can be closest to God in His house. Every Catholic church is God's house because He is in the tabernacle. When we are in church, we must be quiet, and show respect for God. While we are in church, we must pray and pay attention when we are at Mass. We must adore God in the tabernacle.

Do you remember when Jesus spoke to the little children? He loved them so much He did not want them to leave, no matter how tired He was. He loves us so much He wants to stay with us always. He is always with us!

We can visit Jesus at church in the tabernacle. The glowing candle tells us He is there waiting for us to talk to Him. We cannot see Him, but He sees us. Jesus loves us to visit Him there.

Open our minds and hearts, O Lord, so we can know and love You!

1. God always _____.

2. God will never _____.

3. God knows _____.

4. God is all _____ and cannot lie.

5. We can visit Jesus at church in the _____.

The Blessed Trinity

There is only one God, but there are three Persons in one God: the Father, the Son, and the Holy Spirit. We do not understand how this can be. It is a mystery. A mystery is a truth we cannot fully understand. This mystery is called the Blessed Trinity. The Father is God and the First Person of the Blessed Trinity. He is our loving Father Who made us. Our dear Jesus, Who saved us from sin, is God the Second Person of the Blessed Trinity. The Holy Spirit is God the Third Person of the Blessed Trinity. He is also called the Holy Ghost. He sanctifies, or gives us grace. Grace is God's life in our souls. It is a special gift from God to our souls. The Holy Spirit gives us grace to help us to be good.

We make the Sign of the Cross with these words:

In the Name of the Father, and of the Son, and of the Holy Spirit. Amen.

There is only one God. There are three Persons in one God. The three Persons are all equal to each other. They love us in every way. They help us to reach Heaven. God our Heavenly Father made us and watches over us. God the Son is Jesus, Who died for us. He opened the gates of Heaven for us. God the Holy Spirit gives us grace to love and obey God.

The Father is not the Son. The Son is not the Holy Spirit. The Holy Spirit is not the Father. There are not three gods, but one God. Yet, there are three Divine Persons in one God. This is a supernatural mystery. No one on Earth can fully explain it. Although we cannot understand this mystery, we believe it because Jesus told it to us in the Bible.

My God, I believe, I adore, I trust, and I love Thee.
I beg pardon for all those who do not believe, do not adore,
do not trust, and do not love Thee.*

1. We call three Persons in one God the

   _____ _____.

2. A _____ is something we cannot fully understand.

3. When we make the Sign of the _____, we honor the
   Blessed Trinity.

   *Prayer of the angel before the Holy Eucharist at Fatima.

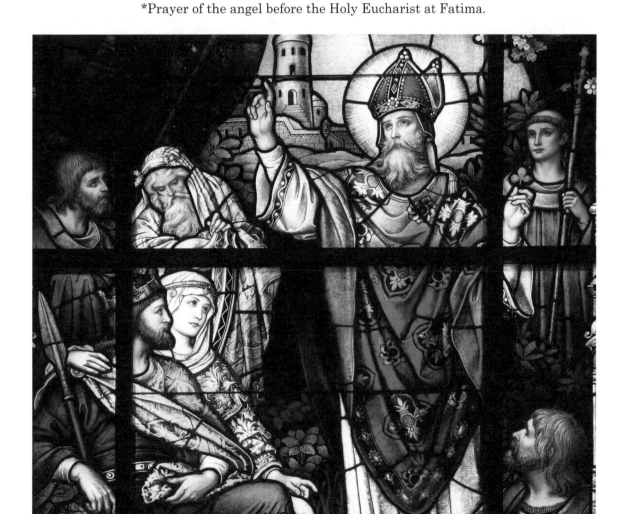

Questions for Week Two

Day 1:

* 1. Does God know all things?

   Yes, God knows all things.

* 2. Did God have a beginning?

   No, God has no beginning and no end. He always was and always will be.

Day 2:

1. Where is God?

   God is everywhere.

2. Where can we visit Jesus?

   We can visit Jesus in any Catholic church. He is in the tabernacle, under the appearance of bread.

Day 3:

1. What do we call the three Persons in one God?

   We call the three Persons in one God the Blessed Trinity: God the Father, God the Son, and God the Holy Spirit.

2. How do we know there are three Persons in one God?

   We know there are three Persons in one God because Jesus revealed it.

3. What is a Divine mystery?

   A Divine mystery is something about our Faith which we cannot fully understand.

Day 4:

* 1. Who is God?

   God is the Supreme Being Who created all things.

* 2. What do we mean when we say that God is the Supreme Being?

   When we say that God is the Supreme Being, we mean that He is above all creatures.

The Angels

God is all good. He is so good that He wants to share His goodness. He created many beautiful creatures called angels. He created them out of nothing. God gave the angels understanding and free will. God created all the angels good.

Angels are pure spirits. They do not have bodies. We cannot see them, but when we see pictures of them, they have wings. We picture them with wings because they can move very quickly from one place to another. When God sends angels down to Earth, God sometimes allows us to see them. Mary could see the angel Gabriel when he visited her to ask her to be the mother of Jesus. Angels are God's messengers.

St. Gabriel, Messenger of God, pray for us.

1. God created the angels out of _____.

2. Angels are pure _____.

3. Angels are God's _____.

God created the angels to love Him and to live with Him forever in Heaven. He gave the angels many gifts. He created them to be the most wonderful and beautiful of all His creatures. They can do things no human person can do. They know more than we can ever know. They will never die. The angels are free to choose right or wrong. That means they have free will.

The angels were very happy and very close to God. The angels were happy to obey God. But some angels became proud. They thought they were too great to serve God. They refused to obey God. This was the first sin. Sin is disobedience to God. The bad angels hated God, even after all He had given them. They rose against Him. Lucifer said, "I will not serve God." He became the leader of the bad angels. The good angels were led by St. Michael. They were faithful to God.

There was a great battle between the good and the bad angels. Because of their sin, Lucifer and the bad angels were cast into Hell forever. We call the bad angels devils. We must guard against Lucifer and the devils, and pray they do not turn us away from God. We should call on St. Michael often and ask his help in not offending God. Pope John Paul II asked us to say this prayer each day:

St. Michael the Archangel, defend us in battle. Be our protection against the wickedness and snares of the devil. May God rebuke him, we humbly pray; and do thou, O Prince of the Heavenly Host, by the divine power of God, cast into Hell Satan and all the evil spirits, who prowl about the world seeking the ruin of souls. Amen.

1. The _____ are the most wonderful of all God's creatures.

2. Angels have _____ will.

3. The leader of the good angels is _____.

4. The leader of the bad angels is _____.

God rewarded St. Michael the Archangel. God rewarded all the good angels. They live happily with God in Heaven. They have many wonderful tasks to do there. Some sing glorious hymns to God. Others surround God's throne and always adore Him. Many are guardian angels.

Each and every one of us has a guardian angel. They pray for us. They watch over us and protect us. They act as messengers from God to us. They help us to stay close to God. They protect us from the devil. They put good thoughts into our minds and strengthen our wills to do good deeds. They protect us from Earthly harm. How wonderful God is to give us a guardian angel all our own. Do you know your Guardian Angel prayer? You should say it every day!

Angel of God, my Guardian Dear,
To whom God's love entrusts me here;
Ever this day, be at my side,
To light and guard, to rule and guide. Amen.

1. God _____ the good angels.

2. Everyone has a _____ _____.

13

Lucifer is the leader of the bad angels. He disobeyed God because of his pride. Lucifer and the bad angels committed a serious sin. Disobedience to God is called sin. Disobedience to God means we think we know better than God does about what we should do.

Lucifer and the other bad angels had to be punished. They were cast into Hell. Today, they are still in Hell. They will be in Hell forever. They are no longer God's friends. The bad angels became devils. They lost their happiness. They are very unhappy because they know they will never again see God and share His happiness.

The bad angels, or devils, do not want us to be God's friends. They do not want us to see God. The bad angels want us to share in their unhappiness. They tempt us to disobey God. Our guardian angels are with us to protect us from the temptations of the devil. That is why we must call on our guardian angels often, especially when it is hard to be good.

My dear Guardian Angel, shield me from harm.

1. Disobedience to God is called _____.

2. The bad angels are in Hell _____.

3. Our _____ angels protect us from the temptations of the devil.

Questions for Week Three

Day 1

   1. What is sin?

      Sin is disobedience to God's Laws.

* 2. Who committed the first sin?

      The bad angels committed the first sin.

* 3. Are angels pure spirits?

      Yes, angels are pure spirits.

Day 2:

* 1. Did all the angels remain faithful to God?

      No, not all the angels remained faithful to God. Some of them sinned.

* 2. What happened to the angels who remained faithful to God?

      The angels who remained faithful to God entered into the eternal happiness of Heaven, and these are called good angels.

   3. Who is the leader of the good angels?

      The leader of the good angels is St. Michael the Archangel.

Day 3:

*   How do the good angels help us?

      The good angels help us by:

         (1) praying for us;

         (2) acting as messengers from God for us; and,

         (3) serving as our guardian angels.

Day 4:

   1. Why can we not see our angels?

      We cannot see our angels because they are spirits.

   2. Who is the leader of the bad angels?

      The leader of the bad angels is Lucifer.

   3. What happened to the angels who disobeyed God?

      The bad angels were cast into the everlasting fires of Hell.

Adam and Eve: Our First Parents

God created the angels. He created the heavens, and then He created the Earth. He created the rivers and the mountains. He created the plants and the animals. Then God created man.

Adam was the first man. Because Adam was alone, God created a wife for him. God created Eve, the first woman. God made them each with a body and a soul. God saw that what He created was very good.

God loved Adam and Eve very much. He gave them many gifts. He gave them the whole Earth and everything in it. They lived in a beautiful place called the Garden of Paradise. God gave them great knowledge. They were free from all sickness and the death of their bodies.

God gave them a very special gift—the greatest gift of all. He gave them Sanctifying Grace. This was the gift of God's own life in them. God gave them another wonderful gift. God made them in the image and likeness of Himself. Sanctifying Grace made them very holy and good. Because of God's great gifts, they tried very hard to be good. They were very close to God in the Garden of Paradise. They talked to God, and God talked to them. Adam and Eve were very happy, and God was very pleased with them.

Teach me, O Lord, to do Your will, for You are my God!

1. God created Adam and Eve with a _____ and a

    _____.

2. God made them in His _____ and _____.

3. God made Adam and Eve free from all _____

    and the _____ of their bodies.

Adam and Eve were very happy living in Paradise. They had Sanctifying Grace. They lived without fear from the animals. They enjoyed all the plants there. It was never too hot or too cold. It was never too wet or too dry. Strong winds never blew. Even the lions and tigers were gentle. All of God's creation was perfect. Did you know that God intended for all of us to live in that beautiful Garden of Paradise? Did you know that our bodies were not supposed to die?

There was a certain tree that grew in the middle of the Garden of Paradise. God called it the Tree of Knowledge of Good and Evil. God told Adam and Eve, "You may eat the fruit of every tree in the Garden except of the Tree of Knowledge of Good and Evil. For the day you eat of this tree, you shall die." God tested our first parents. Like the angels, they had to be tested before they could be with God in Heaven. He wanted to see if they would love and serve Him. Because Adam and Eve obeyed God, they were happy.

O My Jesus, may I never displease You!

1. God called the tree, the Tree of _____ of

   _____ and _____.

2. God _____ Adam and Eve before they could be with Him in Heaven.

One day, Lucifer, the leader of the devils, took the shape of a serpent and visited the Garden of Paradise. He told Eve that if she ate of the Tree of Knowledge of Good and Evil, she would be as great as God. He was jealous of Adam and Eve's friendship with God. He saw how beautiful God had made them in His own image.

Eve believed the devil's lie. The fruit of the tree looked bright and beautiful. She disobeyed God and ate the forbidden fruit. She gave the fruit to Adam. Adam ate it, too. They both disobeyed God. Right away, they both knew they had done wrong. This was the first sin of man. They tried to hide from God, but God sees everything. He knew what they had done, just as He knows everything we do.

The moment Adam and Eve sinned, God's life of grace left their souls. They lost God's greatest gift: Sanctifying Grace. No longer was it easy for them to be good and holy. God sent them out of the beautiful Garden of Paradise. They suffered pain, and their bodies eventually died. They had to work hard to grow food. The animals were no longer gentle. Adam and Eve felt cold and heat. They knew sadness. They grew old. They lost all their beautiful gifts. The gates of Heaven were closed to Adam and Eve and to their children. It was closed to all of us because of our first parents' sin. Adam and Eve were very sorry for what they did. They lived a hard life from then on, trying to make up for their sin of disobedience.

O God, be merciful to me, a sinner!

1. The devil took the shape of a _____.

2. The devil was jealous of Adam and Eve's _____ with God.

3. The moment they sinned, God's life of _____ left their souls.

Adam and Eve were our first parents. Our first parents committed the first sin on Earth. It is called Original Sin. By their sin, they lost all God's wonderful gifts. Because Adam and Eve are everybody's first parents, we are all born without God's Sanctifying Grace. We inherit Adam and Eve's Original Sin and its punishment. Like Adam and Eve, we too must suffer and die.

God loves each person He makes. God did not abandon Adam and Eve in their sinfulness. God helped them to be sorry for their sin. He promised to send a Savior to free them from their sins. This Savior would reopen the gates of Heaven to them. They were sad but they had hope. In their suffering, they would remember God's promise and be comforted. The Savior is God's only Son! He is God and the Second Person of the Blessed Trinity.

God the Son, Jesus Christ, gave us the Sacrament of Baptism. When you were a baby, your parents brought you to church to be baptized. The priest poured water over your head and said special prayers. In Baptism, Original Sin is washed away. In Baptism, we receive Sanctifying Grace.

O Mary, conceived without sin, pray for us who have recourse to thee!

1. Adam's sin in us is called _____ _____.

2. God promised to send a _____.

3. The Sacrament of _____ washes away Original Sin.

Questions for Week Four

Day 1:

1. Who were the first man and woman?

   Adam and Eve were the first man and woman.

2. What was Adam and Eve's greatest gift from God?

   Their greatest gift from God was Sanctifying Grace.

3. What is Sanctifying Grace?

   Sanctifying Grace is the gift of God's own life in our souls.

Day 2:

What did God tell Adam and Eve about the Tree of Knowledge of Good and Evil?

God told Adam and Eve that they were not to eat the fruit of the Tree of the Knowledge of Good and Evil. If they ate its fruit, they would die.

Day 3:

Did Adam and Eve disobey God?

Yes, Adam and Eve disobeyed God.

Day 4:

* 1. Who committed the first sin on Earth?

   Our first parents, Adam and Eve, committed the first sin on Earth.

* 2. Is this sin passed on to us from Adam?

   Yes, this sin is passed on to us from Adam.

* 3. What is this sin in us called?

   This sin in us is called Original Sin.

4. Are we all born with Original Sin?

   Yes, we are all born with Original Sin.

* 5. Was anyone ever free from Original Sin?

   The Blessed Virgin Mary was free from Original Sin.

Actual Sin

The children of Adam and Eve inherited Original Sin.

Cain and Abel were sons of Adam and Eve. Cain worked as a farmer, while Abel was a shepherd. Abel was good and loved God very much. His brother Cain did not love God, and he did not love his brother, either.

Abel built an altar to offer sacrifice as a gift to God. He chose the finest lamb from his flock. Because Abel was good and unselfish in his gift, God was pleased with his sacrifice. Cain offered a sacrifice, too. He gathered some of his crops to offer to God. But Cain kept the best of his crops for himself, and gave the second best to God. God saw this, and was not pleased with Cain's offering.

O My Jesus, I offer You my best gift: obedience to You.

1. The sons of Adam and Eve were _____ and

   _____.

2. _____ was good and unselfish.

3. _____ did not love God or his brother.

When Cain saw that his brother Abel's gift was pleasing to God, he was jealous. Cain became angry and killed Abel. This was a terrible sin. Cain's sin was an actual sin. It was a sin he committed himself.

God knew what Cain had done but asked him where Abel was. Cain answered, "Am I my brother's keeper?" This meant that he did not think himself responsible for his brother's well-being. God punished Cain for his terrible crime. He sent him away from his home. He was forced to wander the Earth for the rest of his life. Cain offended God by destroying the life that God gave Abel.

From all sin, deliver me, O Lord.

1. Cain became very angry and _____ Abel.

2. Cain's sin was an _____ sin.

3. Cain was forced to _____ the Earth.

When Cain killed his brother Abel, he committed an actual sin. Actual sin is any willful thought, desire, word, action, or omission forbidden by the Law of God. Actual sin is any sin that we ourselves commit. Actual sin is a sin of disobedience to God's Laws.

If I willingly do something that God's Commandments tells me is wrong, then I commit an actual sin. To willingly think mean thoughts is sinful. For instance, if a boy stumbles and falls, and I say to myself, "It serves him right," I am being unkind to him in my thoughts. This is disobeying God's Law to "love thy neighbor as thyself."

If I willingly desire something sinful, and would commit the sin if I could get away with it, then I commit a sin. If I want to steal someone's bicycle, and would if no one were looking, that is a sinful desire.

If I willingly say things that are bad or mean, then those words are sinful. It is sinful to tell a lie. It is sinful to talk back to my parents. It is sinful to use Our Lord's holy name of Jesus in a wrong way.

If I willingly do something that I know is wrong or bad, then I commit an actual sin. If I am mean to my brothers or sisters and hurt them, then I commit an actual sin. Sometimes, we do something bad suddenly without thinking, just because we are suddenly angry. Without full consent of the will, that is not a sin.

If I willingly refuse to do something that God's Law tells me I must do, then I commit an actual sin. This kind of sin is a sin of omission. This means that a sin is committed by *not doing* something. If I do not go to Mass on Sunday because I want to sleep very late, then I commit an actual sin of omission.

Immaculate Heart of Mary,
pray for us now and at the hour of our death.

1. Actual sin is any willful _____, _____,

   _____, _____, or

   _____ forbidden by the Law of God.

2. If I do not do something that God's Law tells me I must do, then I

   commit a sin of _____.

Actual sins are sins we actually commit ourselves. Not all actual sins are equally bad. There are two kinds of actual sins: mortal sin and venial sin.

Mortal sin is a serious offense against the Law of God. The word "mortal" means deadly. If we eat food that is poisonous, we die. Mortal sin is poison to our soul. If we commit a mortal sin, God's life of grace dies in our soul. This does not mean that our souls die, because our souls will live forever. When we commit a mortal sin, we take away God's Sanctifying Grace from our soul. We are no longer God's friend. If we commit a mortal sin, we become an enemy of God. If we commit a mortal sin, then we do not love God. There is a terrible punishment for mortal sin. If we die with mortal sin on our souls, we shall never see God, and we shall go to Hell forever. To murder someone, for example, is a mortal sin. Soldiers killing in war, or someone killing an attacker is usually not a sin.

Venial sin is a less serious offense against the Law of God. Venial sin does not rob our soul of Sanctifying Grace. We are still friends of God. Venial sin does not drive God from our souls, but venial sin offends God, Who loves us very much. Venial sin makes us less pleasing to God. Venial sin brings punishment as well. Committing many venial sins will make us love God less and less. Worst of all, repeating venial sins can make it easy for us to commit mortal sin. That is why we should try very hard to keep away from even the smallest venial sin. Stealing a small amount of candy is an example of a venial sin.

Lamb of God, Who takes away the sins of the world, have mercy on us!

1. There are two kinds of actual sin: _____ and

   _____.

2. Mortal sin makes us an _____ of God.

3. Venial sin is a _____ serious sin.

Questions for Week Five

Day 1

1. Who were the sons of Adam and Eve?

   Cain and Abel were the sons of Adam and Eve.

2. Where do we learn the story of Cain and Abel?

   We learn the story of Cain and Abel from the Bible.

* 3. Is Original Sin the only kind of sin?

   No, there is another kind of sin, called actual sin.

Day 2

1. Why was Abel's sacrifice pleasing to God?

   Abel's sacrifice was pleasing to God because Abel gave his best to God.

2. What happened when Cain saw that God was pleased with his brother's sacrifice but not with his?

   Cain became jealous and murdered his brother Abel.

Day 3

* 1. What is actual sin?

   Actual sin is any sin which we ourselves commit.

2. What is a sin of omission?

   A sin of omission is not doing something which God's Law says must be done.

Day 4

* 1. How many kinds of actual sin are there?

   There are two kinds of actual sin: mortal sin and venial sin.

* 2. What is mortal sin?

   Mortal sin is a deadly sin. It is a serious and deliberate disobedience to a Law of God.

* 3. What does mortal sin do to us?

   Mortal sin makes us enemies of God and robs our souls of His grace.

* 4. What is venial sin?

   Venial sin is a lesser sin.

Moses and the Ten Commandments

After Adam and Eve sinned, God promised He would send them a Savior. The Savior would free them and all the people who would live in the world in the future. The Savior would reopen the gates of Heaven.

God watched over His Chosen People, who were called Jews. From the Jewish people, Christ the Savior would be born.

For 430 years, the Jews lived in the land of Egypt. A good Egyptian king invited the Jews to live in Egypt during a famine. Later, an evil man became king. He treated the Jewish people cruelly and made them work in slavery, but God was watching over His people. He sent them a great prophet to deliver them from the hands of the Egyptian king. His name was Moses. A prophet is a man chosen by God to give God's messages to His people.

Moses led God's Chosen People from Egypt, and they were very thankful to God. However, the Chosen People were weak. They suffered from Original Sin. Soon after they were delivered from Egypt, they forgot about God and disobeyed Him. They committed many sins. Then God gave Moses the Ten Commandments so that they would know how He wanted them to live. The Ten Commandments are for everyone.

Things to Remember about Obeying God's Commandments:

1. We show our love for God by obeying Him.

2. We offend God if we disobey Him.

3. We should think often about how much God loves us.

4. If we commit a sin, we should immediately tell God we are sorry for offending Him, because we love Him so much.

St. Joseph, model of every virtue, pray for us.

1. _____ delivered God's Chosen People from the Egyptians.

2. God gave Moses the _____ _____ to show how He wants people to live.

Do you know the story of Moses and the Burning Bush? Moses went up Mount Sinai and saw a burning bush. The bush was on fire, but the branches were not consumed, or burned. Out of the burning bush came the voice of God! God told Moses to take off his sandals because he was on holy ground.

Later, God told Moses that He wanted to make a covenant with His people. A covenant is a very special agreement. God said, "I shall be your God, and you shall be My people." God told Moses to say to the Jewish people, "Keep My Commandments, and someday I shall send a Savior." God carved the Ten Commandments onto two stone tablets and gave them to Moses. God chose the Jews to give the world and all of us the Ten Commandments.

These Commandments are very important. We must memorize all ten of them and learn what they mean so that we can know how God wants us to live.

Holy Angel, my protector, help me to keep God's Commandments.

1. Moses took off his shoes because he was on _____ ground.

2. God made a _____ with His people.

3. God said, "Keep my _____."

The First Commandment:
"I am the Lord thy God. Thou shalt not have strange gods before Me."

Back in the time of Moses, only the Jews, the Chosen People, knew about the True God. In Egypt, where the Jews lived, the people did not know the True God. The Egyptians worshiped false gods represented by statues or idols. Usually, an idol was a statue of an animal. Sometimes the Chosen People in their sinfulness would forget about the True God and worship these idols, too! This was a mortal sin.

Today, almost everyone knows there is only one God. Can we still break the First Commandment by having "false gods"? If people care more about money than they do about God, they are breaking the First Commandment.

There are many other ways we can break this Commandment, too. Do we continue to play when it is time to say our prayers?

By making something more important than God, or more important than the worship of God, we break the First Commandment. The First Commandment of God is: "I am the Lord thy God. Thou shalt not have strange gods before Me."

My Patron Saint, help me to know, love, and serve God.

1. Long ago, the Egyptians worshipped _____ gods.

2. Only the Chosen People worshipped the _____ God.

3. "I am the Lord thy God. Thou shalt not have _____

    _____ before Me."

The Second Commandment:
"Thou shalt not take the Name of the Lord thy God in vain."

God says we must love Him with our whole heart, our whole soul, our whole mind, and our whole strength. Each time we speak or hear the Holy Name of our dear Jesus, we should bow our heads to show our love and respect.

Whenever we pray, we must mean what we say. We must think about God when we pray. We kneel. We make the Sign of the Cross. God listens to our prayers. Our dear Lord is offended if we play in church. We must always speak with reverence of the saints and of all holy things.

The Name of Jesus is very powerful! The Bible tells us that once St. Peter said to a man who could not walk, "In the Name of Jesus Christ, arise and walk!" Right away, the man got up and walked. What a wonderful God our dear Jesus is! What respect His Name deserves!

The Second Commandment of God is: "Thou shalt not take the Name of the Lord thy God in vain."

Let us bow our heads and pray:

Praised and blessed forever be the Holy Name of Jesus!

1. We should bow our _____ when we hear the Holy Name of Jesus.

2. Thou shalt not take the _____ of the Lord thy God in vain.

Questions for Week Six

Day 1

What did God give Moses to show how He wants people to live?

God gave Moses the Ten Commandments to show how He wants people to live.

Day 2:

What was the agreement that God made with His Chosen People?

The agreement that God made with His Chosen People was, "I shall be your God, and you shall by My people."

Day 3:

1. What is the First Commandment of God?

   The First Commandment is, "I am the Lord thy God. Thou shalt not have strange gods before Me."

2. What are some false gods?

   A false god refers to anything which a person treats as more important than obeying God. This could be money, or a car, or a job, for example.

Day 4:

1. What is the Second Commandment of God?

   The Second Commandment is, "Thou shalt not take the Name of the Lord thy God in vain."

2. How should we speak of God?

   We must speak of God with reverence.

3. What does the Second Commandment tell us we must do?

   The Second Commandment tells us we must speak with reverence about God, His Blessed Mother, the saints, and all holy things.

The Third, Fourth, Fifth, and Sixth Commandments

The Third Commandment: "Remember, keep holy the Lord's Day."

The Third Commandment tells us that Sunday is a special day set aside for God. After our morning prayers, we start our Sunday with the Holy Sacrifice of the Mass. We *can* go to Mass on other days. We *must* attend Sunday Mass. We are commanded to show God proper worship on Sunday. It was on Sunday that Jesus rose from the dead. It was also on Sunday that the Holy Spirit came. This special feast day called Pentecost is the birthday of the Church.

We must take care to dress in our best clothes for Mass to show our love for God. Wearing our best clothes shows God that we honor and respect His holy day. We should be at Mass on time and be in our place before Mass begins. We must not talk, laugh, or look around in church. In this way, we will honor God's special day and keep His Commandment.

Sunday is also the day that God has set aside for us to rest and enjoy with our families. The Bible tells us that after God created Adam, He rested on the seventh day. Since the Third Commandment tells us to keep the day holy, the Church has told us not to do any unnecessary work on Sundays, especially work which is for hire or for pay, or work which requires labor of body rather than of mind. Some special people must work on Sundays. Policemen, firemen, doctors, and nurses are some of the people who must work on Sundays. The jobs of these people are to take care of us and keep us safe.

Normal work for our family on Sundays is necessary, such as cooking or making our beds. We should avoid all unnecessary shopping. Our Lord wants us to rest with our families and take extra time to think of Him, to talk to Him, and to thank Him for His goodness.

Blessed be His most Sacred Heart!

1. _____ is a special day set aside for God.

2. We must not do any unnecessary _____ on Sundays.

3. Unnecessary work is work of the _____ rather than of the mind.

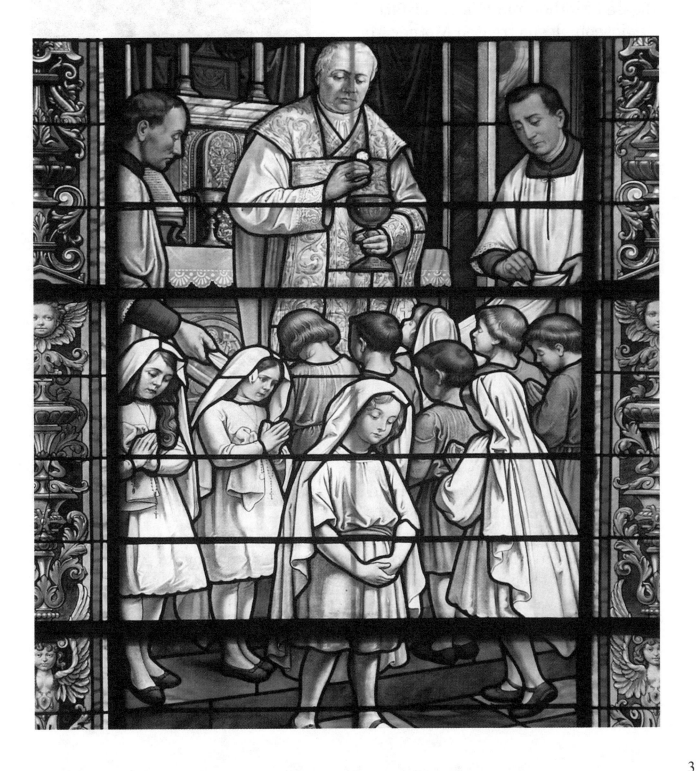

The Fourth Commandment: "Honor thy Father and thy Mother."

We love our parents. We must always obey, honor, and respect them. In this way, we show we love God and our parents. When Jesus lived on Earth, He always lovingly obeyed His Blessed Mother and His foster-father, St. Joseph. Jesus treated Mother Mary and St. Joseph with honor and respect. He never talked back. He helped them even before they asked. Jesus spent many years showing us how to obey the Fourth Commandment. God made us, and chose our mother and father for us.

Think of ways you can help your parents before they ask. You could put away your toys, clean your room, make your bed, carry the dirty dishes to the sink, or help with your younger brothers and sisters. How happy we make our parents when we obey them! How happy we make our parents when we help them with chores around the house. How happy we make Jesus, too. In these ways, we show Jesus and our parents that we love them.

Our parents love us and want what is best for us. They try hard to take care of us. Father works to earn money to buy the things we need. Mother takes loving care of us from the time we are babies. Our parents teach us about Jesus and show us how to get to Heaven. Our parents teach us how to read and write. They teach us arithmetic and other things we need to know. We must pray to God for our parents. They need many graces to raise a family.

The Fourth Commandment also tells us we must respect and obey all those who take the place of our parents. We must respect and obey our grandparents and our other relatives. Sometimes our parents tell us to obey an older brother or sister, an uncle or an aunt, or a friend. We should do what they say in a polite and kind way. We must do our school lessons carefully and be obedient. We must honor the good priests, sisters, and brothers, the religious who have given their lives to Our Lord. God wants us to show respect for all who are in charge of us.

Sweet Heart of Jesus, be my salvation.

1. By the Fourth Commandment we are commanded to

   _____, _____, and _____ our parents.

2. The Fourth Commandment tells us to _____ all those who take the place of our parents.

3. We must honor _____ who have given their lives to Our Lord, such as priest and nuns.

The Fifth Commandment: "Thou shalt not kill."

God tells us to love our neighbors as ourselves. Our Lord Jesus loved even His enemies. When they nailed Him to the Cross, Our Lord said, "Father, forgive them for they do not know what they do." Jesus Christ forgave His enemies. He did not hate them. We too must try to be like Jesus. We must never hate anyone. It is sinful to be selfish, or to fight. We must not fight with our brothers and sisters. We must also control our anger. We may never act unjustly or unkindly. If we do any of these things, then we are breaking the Fifth Commandment. We must hate only evil. We must not hate the person who does evil.

Do you remember the story of Cain and Abel? Abel was a good son. He worked hard and prayed. He always did his best to please God. His brother Cain was not close to God. He did not try to give his best for God. He was selfish and lazy. One day, he became so jealous and angry at his brother Abel that he killed him! What a horrible sin! Jealousy and anger make us lose God's grace.

The Fifth Commandment of God tells us to be kind to others. It also tells us to take care of our bodies and our souls and of the bodies and souls of our neighbors. We must not argue and become angry, or yell in anger. We must not hit anyone, or hurt anyone. In this way we are keeping God's Fifth Commandment. We must always do good to show others how to do good. When we do good, we show we love God and our neighbor.

O Jesus, meek and humble of heart,
make my heart like unto Thine.

1. Our Lord prayed, "Father, _____ them, for they do not know what they do."

2. We must hate _____ but not the person who does evil.

3. When Cain killed his brother Abel, he broke the _____ Commandment.

The Sixth Commandment: "Thou shalt not commit adultery."

The Sixth Commandment tells us to keep our words, looks, and actions clean and pure. Mary, our Blessed Mother, was truly pure. She did not have the slightest stain of Original Sin. During her whole life, she never did an evil or impure thing. Jesus and Mary want us to stay clean and pure. Sin makes our souls impure and displeasing to God. Prayer and being good make our souls clean and pure.

In order to keep our souls clean, we need to pray to our Blessed Lady every day and ask her for help. We must stay away from things that may make us sin. Bad television shows and commercials give us bad ideas. Bad movies or bad companions may put evil ideas into our heads. We must be careful to dress modestly. Our guardian angels will protect us if we pray to them and stay away from sin. Remember to pray the Guardian Angel prayer every day:

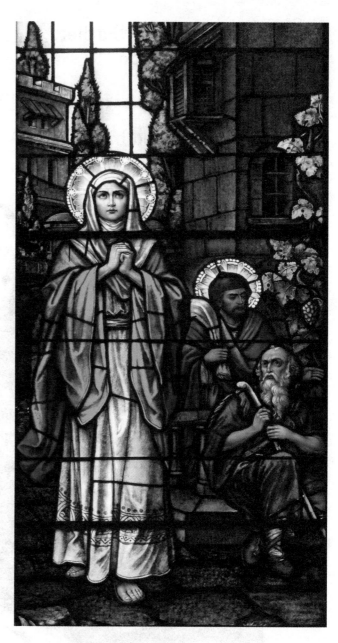

Angel of God, my Guardian dear,
To whom God's love entrusts me here,
Ever this day, be at my side
To light and guard, to rule and guide. Amen.

Keep a picture or statue of Our Lord or His Blessed Mother in your room. If we try to imitate Jesus and be Mary-like in the way we dress and act, then being pure will be a way of life for us. Let us fill our minds with good thoughts and keep our souls pure!

Saint Maria Goretti, pray for us.

1. The Sixth Commandment tells us to keep our words, looks, and actions _____ and _____.

2. In order to stay pure, we should pray to our _____ _____ every day.

3. We should imitate Jesus and _____ in the way we dress and act.

Questions for Week Seven

Day 1:

* 1. What is the Third Commandment of God?

     The Third Commandment of God is, "Remember, keep holy the Lord's Day."

  2. What things should we do to keep Sunday holy?

     On Sunday, we should go to Mass, spend time with our family, rest, and think about God more often than usual.

  3. What things should we not do on Sunday?

     On Sunday, we should not do any unnecessary work.

Day 2:

* 1. What is the Fourth Commandment of God?

     The Fourth Commandment of God is, "Honor thy Father and thy Mother."

  2. What does the Fourth Commandment command us to do?

     The Fourth Commandment commands us to respect and show love for our parents, to obey them in all that is not sinful, and to help them when they are in need.

  3. How did Jesus treat His mother and Saint Joseph?

     Jesus always obeyed His mother and St. Joseph and treated them with love and respect.

Day 3:

* 1. What is the Fifth Commandment of God?

     The Fifth Commandment of God is, "Thou shall not kill."

  2. What are we commanded by the Fifth Commandment ?

     By the Fifth Commandment, we are commanded to be kind and loving to everyone, our enemies as well as our friends. We must not fight with or hate others.

Day 4:

* 1. What is the Sixth Commandment of God?

     The Sixth Commandment of God is, "Thou shall not commit adultery."

  2. What are we commanded by the Sixth Commandment?

     By the Sixth Commandment, we are commanded to be pure in all our words, looks, and actions.

The Seventh, Eighth, Ninth, and Tenth Commandments

The Seventh Commandment: "Thou shalt not steal."

The Seventh Commandment is, "Thou shalt not steal." Stealing can be a grave sin. Even if we think taking something little could not hurt anyone, we are wrong. Jesus and our guardian angel want us to be good and responsible. If we borrow a library book, we must return it on time. If we want some candy, a toy, or a new pencil in a store, we must pay for it.

Jesus wants us to be responsible with other people's things. If we borrow something, we must return it. If we break it, we should repair it or replace it. We must always ask before we borrow something.

Stealing something little is a venial sin that can lead to worse sins. Judas Iscariot was one of the twelve Apostles. He took care of all the money that the Apostles had so that they could buy food for themselves and for Jesus. They gave most of their money to the poor. At first, Judas started stealing a little bit of money. He soon became so greedy that he betrayed Jesus. He turned Jesus over to His enemies for thirty pieces of silver. What a horrible sin! Pray that your guardian angel will protect you from the sin of stealing.

We also can break God's Seventh Commandment by cheating. If we cheat at a game or on a test, then we are taking something that does not belong to us. The Seventh Commandment tells us to be honest and not to steal, cheat, or damage the property of others.

**Dear Jesus, in all I think and do and say,
Help me to be honest each and every day.**

1. The Seventh Commandment is "Thou shalt not _____."

2. If we borrow something, then we must _____ it in good condition.

3. The Seventh Commandment tells us to be _____ and not to steal, cheat, or _____ the property of others.

The Eighth Commandment:
"Thou shalt not bear false witness against thy neighbor."

The Eighth Commandment teaches us that we must not lie. Bearing false witness against our neighbor is telling a lie about someone else. Sometimes it is hard to tell the truth. It is hard to tell our parents if we have broken something or have done something wrong. Remember, Jesus sees everything. He knows when we do wrong. It pleases Him very much if we are sorry and we tell the truth, especially if it is hard for us.

The Eighth Commandment of God forbids us to harm the good name of another. All of us want to be liked and respected. That is what having a good name means. If our good name is taken away by someone, then people will turn against us. That will hurt us. It is wrong to steal a person's money, but it is also wrong to steal someone's good name. Even if we are telling the truth, we must be careful to be kind. We should not talk about the faults of others because we might harm their good name. Unless we have a very good reason, it is sinful to tell bad things about others even if they are true! We should ask our parents for advice when we think we have a good reason. Pray that your guardian angel will help you always to speak well of others.

I love my neighbor as myself for the love of Thee, my Jesus.

1. Thou shalt not bear _____ _____ against thy neighbor.

2. We must never tell a _____.

3. Unless we have a good reason, such as telling our parents, it is

   sinful to tell _____ things about others, even if they are true.

The Ninth and Tenth Commandments:

"Thou shalt not covet thy neighbor's wife."
"Thou shalt not covet thy neighbor's goods."

We always need to keep our thoughts pure and good, not just our actions. These two Commandments tell us always to keep our thoughts about others good. To covet means to want something very, very much that belongs to someone else. We should be happy in the good fortune of others and be satisfied with what we have. Jesus has given us something so much more important than toys or clothes. When we receive Jesus in Holy Communion, He shares His life with us. If we stay in God's grace, then we shall be in Heaven with God someday.

When we love others, we are glad for them. It is wrong to be jealous of your friends for what they may have. It is wrong to be envious of your friend because he has a new bike. We should not trouble our parents to buy us toys or candy each time they take us to the store. We should be thankful for all they have provided for us. We must remember that our parents work hard to give us what we have. We must remember to thank God in our prayers each night for all the good things He has given us. We should remember that there are many children who do not have all the good things we have. We must ask our dear Lord to bless all those who are less fortunate than we are. We must remember that all good things come from God, and that He always gives us what is best for us.

O my God, I love Thee above all things.

1. The Ninth Commandment tells us that our _____ must be pure and good.

2. We should be happy about the good fortune of others and be

   _____ with what we have.

3. To _____ means to want very much something that belongs to someone else.

Questions for Week Eight

Day 1:

* 1. What is the Seventh Commandment of God?
     The Seventh Commandment of God is, "Thou shalt not steal."

  2. What does the Seventh Commandment tell us to do?
     The Seventh Commandment tells us we must not take anything that does not belong to us, no matter how small.

Day 2:

* 1. What is the Eighth Commandment of God?
     The Eighth Commandment of God is, "Thou shalt not bear false witness against thy neighbor."

  2. What does the Eighth Commandment tell us to do?
     The Eighth Commandment commands us always to tell the truth, no matter how hard it may be.

  3. Who always knows when we lie?
     God always knows when we lie.

Day 3:

* 1. What is the Ninth Commandment of God?
     The Ninth Commandment of God is, "Thou shalt not covet thy neighbor's wife."

  2. What does the Ninth Commandment command of us?
     By the Ninth Commandment we are commanded to be pure in our thoughts and desires.

* 3. What is the Tenth Commandment of God?
     The Tenth Commandment of God is, "Thou shalt not covet thy neighbor's goods."

* 4. What does the Tenth Commandment forbid?
     The Tenth Commandment forbids all desire to take or to keep unjustly what belongs to others, and forbids envy at their success.

Day 4:

1. What are the Ten Commandments of God?

   The Commandments of God are these ten:

   I. I am the Lord thy God. Thou shalt not have strange gods before Me.

   II. Thou shalt not take the name of the Lord thy God in vain.

   III. Remember, keep holy the Lord's Day.

   IV. Honor thy father and thy mother.

   V. Thou shalt not kill.

   VI. Thou shalt not commit adultery.

   VII. Thou shalt not steal.

   VIII. Thou shalt not bear false witness against thy neighbor.

   IX. Thou shalt not covet thy neighbor's wife.

   X. Thou shalt not covet thy neighbor's goods.

2. Memorize and recite the Ten Commandments.

First Quarter Review

WEEK NINE: Day 1   Review work from Weeks 1, 2, and 3

WEEK NINE: Day 2   Review work from Weeks 4, 5, and 6

WEEK NINE: Day 3   Review work from Weeks 7 and 8

WEEK NINE: Day 4   Take First Quarter Test

Note: If extra time is needed, use Day 4 to review. Use Day 5 to take the test.

48

Second Quarter

God Sends His Son

God's Goodness

After God gave the Ten Commandments to Moses, there were still many, many years that would pass before God would send the Savior. There were many good people who waited for the Savior to come. The Chosen People, the Jews, prayed and prayed. They tried to live good lives by keeping God's Commandments. They remembered His promise to send a Redeemer, and they prepared themselves for His Coming.

Finally, many years after the time of Adam's fall, God the Father sent the Savior to His people. He sent His only Son to become Man and to live on Earth. Jesus was born on the first Christmas Day, over two thousand years ago. Jesus came to do His Father's Will, to open the gates of Heaven for us, and to teach us how to live.

Each year, we remember in a special way how the Chosen People waited for God's promise to be fulfilled. We prepare our hearts for the Savior's coming. Advent is that holy time when we wait and prepare ourselves to celebrate the birth of Jesus at Christmas. We spend this holy time saying special prayers and lighting special candles. In this way, we remember that God always keeps His promises. In this way, we prepare the way of the Lord.

O Divine Infant Jesus,
prepare my heart for Your dwelling place.

1. God the Father promised to send a _____.

2. Jesus, God's only Son, became _____.

3. Jesus came to do His Father's _____.

4. We call the holy time of waiting for Christ's coming

_____.

Finally, the time came for God to send His Son to be the Savior of the world. God chose a very special way to send His Son. He sent His Son to us as a Baby born of the Blessed Virgin Mary. She was pure and good. She did not have Original Sin.

God gave to Mary all the holy graces that He gave to Eve, and many more. Mary was much more careful than Eve with the precious gifts God gave her. Unlike Eve, she did not fall into sin. In fact, she did not have any stain of sin at all.

Mary was full of Sanctifying Grace, even before she was born. Mary loved God with her whole heart, soul, and mind. Her soul was perfectly pleasing to God in every way. She was filled with grace. That is why we pray, "Hail Mary, full of grace."

God gave Mary to us as our Heavenly Mother. She helps us to be pure and good. Our Blessed Mother loves us very much and wants to help us go to Heaven. Our Lord Jesus wants us to pray to His Blessed Mother every day.

Heavenly Mother, show me the way to Jesus.

1. Jesus was born of the _____ _____ _____.

2. Our Lady is free from every kind of _____.

3. "Hail Mary, full of _____."

When Mary was about fourteen years old, she had a special visitor. She was praying alone in her room when, suddenly, the beautiful Archangel Gabriel appeared before her. He was sent from God to give Mary a message. Gabriel knew that Mary pleased God more than any person He had ever created. Gabriel knew she had never offended God by even the smallest sin. Gabriel knew that she was full of grace. Gabriel said to Mary,

"Hail, full of grace, the Lord is with thee.

Do you recognize the angel's greeting to Mary? They are the first words of the Hail Mary prayer.

Mary was surprised at first. She told the Archangel Gabriel that she would do whatever God wanted. She said, "Behold the handmaid of the Lord. Be it done unto me according to thy word." God wanted her to be the Mother of His Son on Earth. We, too, must do God's Will without question, just as Mary did. Let us ask Our Lady to help us. When we love God, we want to do His Will.

Holy Mary, Mother of God, pray for us sinners.

1. The Archangel _____ appeared to Mary.

2. The angel was sent by God to give Mary a _____.

3. Mary never _____ God by even the smallest sin.

The Archangel Gabriel came to announce to Mary the good news about the coming of the Savior. He told her that she was most pleasing to God because of her complete goodness. He told her she was to be the Mother of the Redeemer! The Archangel Gabriel told her that the Child's Name was to be Jesus and He would save His people from their sins! On this very special day, the Archangel Gabriel told the Blessed Virgin Mary that her Child would be the Son of God. Because he made such a wonderful announcement, we call this important day, "The Feast of the Annunciation." Each year, the Catholic Church remembers and honors the wonderful things that happened that day, over two thousand years ago.

The Archangel Gabriel then told Mary that her cousin Elizabeth also was to have a baby. Our Lady quickly went to visit Elizabeth to share their joy. Since Elizabeth was much older, Mary wanted to help her get ready for the new baby. When Elizabeth met her cousin Mary, something marvelous happened: Elizabeth's baby leapt in her womb! Then, Elizabeth, filled with the Holy Spirit, said excitedly to Our Lady,

"Blessed art thou among women,
and blessed is the Fruit of thy womb!"

Do you recognize these words? They make up the next part of the Hail Mary prayer. Elizabeth also said, "Who am I that the Mother of my Lord should come to me?" Elizabeth knew that Mary's Baby would be the Savior for whom the Jews had been waiting since the sin of Adam. The Church honors this miraculous event on a special feast day we call "The Visitation."

Elizabeth named her baby John. When he became older, the people knew him as John the Baptist. John was sent by God for a special mission. He was to prepare the way of the Lord. John was to tell everyone about Jesus and get them ready for the coming of the promised Redeemer! Today, St. John the Baptist is a very special saint in Heaven.

Prepare the way of the Lord. Make straight His paths!

1. We honor the Archangel Gabriel's visit to Mary on the Feast of the _____.

2. We honor Mary's visit to her cousin Elizabeth on the Feast of the _____.

3. Elizabeth's baby was St. _____ the Baptist.

Questions for Week Ten

Day 1

* 1. Did one of the Persons of the Blessed Trinity become man?

Yes, the Second Person, the Son of God, became man.

2. When did the Second Person of the Blessed Trinity become man?

The Second Person of the Blessed Trinity became man in the womb of the Blessed Virgin Mary when she agreed to be the Mother of God. This happened when the Archangel Gabriel appeared to her.

* 3. What is the Name of the Son of God made man?

The Name of the Son of God made man is Jesus Christ.

4. What is the name of the holy season when we prepare for the coming of the Savior?

The holy season when we prepare for the coming of the Savior is Advent.

* 5. When was Jesus born?

Jesus was born on the first Christmas Day, over two thousand years ago.

Day 2

* 1. Who is the Mother of Jesus?

   The Mother of Jesus is the Blessed Virgin Mary.

* 2. Is Jesus Christ both God and man?

   Yes, Jesus Christ is both God and man.

Day 3

1. Who was the archangel who appeared to Mary?

   The Archangel Gabriel appeared to Mary.

2. What did the Archangel Gabriel say to Mary?

   Gabriel said, "Hail, full of grace, the Lord is with thee."

Day 4

1. What event do we honor on the Feast of the Annunciation?

   On the Annunciation, we honor the Archangel Gabriel announcing to Mary that she was to be the Mother of the Savior, Jesus Christ.

2. What event do we honor on the Feast of the Visitation?

   On the Feast of the Visitation, we honor Mary's meeting with her cousin Elizabeth.

The Birth of Jesus

God chose the Blessed Virgin Mary to be the Mother of Jesus. God chose St. Joseph to be the head and protector of the Holy Family. God chose St. Joseph to be the foster-father of Jesus.

St. Joseph was a carpenter. He was patient, hard-working, and very holy. He obeyed God and took good care of Mary. In their happy home in Nazareth, Mary and Joseph waited for the Son of God to be born.

However, Our Lord Jesus was not born in Nazareth. At that time, the Roman emperor wanted to count all the people of his empire. That is called a census. All the people of the Roman Empire, including Mary and Joseph, were ordered to register in the home town of their ancestors. Since Mary and Joseph were both from the house and family of King David, they went to the City of David, which was Bethlehem. This was not easy for Mary and Joseph because Bethlehem was very far away. It was hard to travel because Mary was soon to have Baby Jesus. Mary rode a donkey while Joseph walked beside her. It was a long and hard trip. Finally, they reached Bethlehem. When they came to an inn, the owner said, "We have no room for you!" All the inns were full, and there was no room for the Holy Family anywhere in the town.

Holy Family, help me to treasure what is truly important in this world.

1. St. Joseph was the _____-_____ of Jesus.

2. St. Joseph worked as a _____.

3. Mary and Joseph had to travel to _____.

When Joseph and Mary reached Bethlehem, Jesus was about to be born. Joseph and Mary could find no room in any of the inns. St. Joseph could find only a cave outside of town. The cave was used as a stable by shepherds, but the Holy Family stayed there. Here, Baby Jesus was born. His bed was a manger filled with straw. Jesus, our Savior, God the Second Person of the Blessed Trinity, chose to be born in a stable in Bethlehem.

Jesus did not choose a king's fine palace. On that first Christmas night, that poor little stable was more wonderful than the world's richest palace. God sent His angels to tell the shepherds the Good News. An angel appeared to them and said:

"Fear not, for behold, I bring you good tidings of great joy that shall be for all the people. For this day in the city of David, is born to you a Savior, Who is Christ the Lord. And this shall be a sign unto you: You shall find the Infant wrapped in swaddling clothes and laid in a manger."

Suddenly, many more angels appeared, and they began to praise God singing, "Glory to God in the highest, and on Earth peace to men of good will." The shepherds hurried through the darkness to the cave, where they found Mary and Joseph, and the Baby Jesus wrapped in swaddling clothes and lying in a manger, just as the angel had told them. They knelt next to Joseph and Mary to adore the Baby Son of God.

Glory to God in the highest!

1. Mary and Joseph went to a cave, because there was no room in

   the _____.

2. Angels appeared to the poor _____ to tell them about the birth of the Savior.

3. Baby Jesus was wrapped in swaddling clothes and laid in a

   _____.

Do you know when Jesus was born? He was born in the early hours of the first Christmas Day. We celebrate His birthday on December 25. On Christmas Eve, the night before Christmas, we prepare for Our Lord's birth in a very special way. We say special prayers. We can hardly wait for Our Lord's birthday to come! Some churches have a special Mass at midnight to welcome Our Lord's special day. Perhaps when you are a little older, your parents will take you to Midnight Mass. On Christmas Day, we go to Holy Mass and sing Christmas songs of joy and praise. The altar is filled with flowers and candles. We give and receive gifts in honor of Baby Jesus' Birthday. We celebrate with our family and friends because it is the day of Our Savior's birth! Most importantly, we thank Jesus for all that He has given us, especially for our family. What can we give to Jesus on His Birthday?

Most adorable Infant Jesus, I give You my heart.

1. Jesus was born on the first _____ Day.

2. We celebrate Christmas on _____ _____.

3. We should thank Jesus for all He has given us, especially for our

   _____.

The Jewish people were not the only ones waiting for Jesus. Three Wise Men from the East were waiting also. They knew that a special star would lead them to the King of kings. They had watched for the star every night. They followed it all the way to Bethlehem. Their journey was long and hard, but they knew that this King was far more special than any Earthly king!

When they found Jesus, the Three Wise Men knelt to adore Him. They brought Him precious gifts of gold, frankincense, and myrrh. All three gifts had a special meaning. Gold, beautiful and costly, showed that Jesus was a great King. Frankincense was used in the Temple by the priests to honor God. The gift of frankincense showed that the kings knew that Jesus Christ is God. Myrrh was a fragrant oil used to prepare bodies for burial. Myrrh showed that Jesus came into the world to suffer and die for our sins.

The Three Wise Men found the Christ Child under the light of a bright star. We can find Jesus under the light of the candle that burns before the tabernacle in church. Make a special visit to Jesus in the tabernacle. That is one of the best Christmas gifts you can give to Jesus! Make a special sacrifice to be with Jesus each Christmas to show Him how much you really love Him!

O Jesus, Friend of little children, bless all the children of the world.

1. The Three Wise Men followed a special _____.

2. They brought Jesus gifts of _____,

   _____, and _____.

3. We can visit Jesus in the _____ of our church.

59

Questions for Week Eleven

Day 1

1. Who was St. Joseph?

   St. Joseph was the husband of Mary and the foster-father of Jesus.

2. Where was Jesus born?

   Jesus was born in a stable in Bethlehem.

3. Why was Jesus born in a stable?

   Jesus was born in a stable because there was no room in the inn.

Day 2

1. Who were the first to learn of the Savior's birth?

   The poor shepherds were the first to learn of the Savior's birth.

2. How did the shepherds learn of the Savior's birth?

   An angel appeared to the shepherds and told them of the Savior's birth.

Day 3

When do we celebrate Our Savior's birth?

We celebrate Our Savior's birth on Christmas Day, December 25.

Day 4

1. Who saw the star in the East?

   The Three Wise Men saw the star in the East.

2. What gifts did the Wise Men bring Jesus?

   The Wise Men brought Jesus gifts of gold, frankincense, and myrrh.

The Holy Family

When the Three Wise Men arrived in Jerusalem, the star disappeared. They asked the people, "Where is the new King? We have seen His star in the East. We have come to worship Him."

King Herod learned of the news. This wicked king worried that the new King would take away his Earthly throne. He worried that the new King's soldiers would take away his kingdom. He summoned the Wise Men to his palace in Jerusalem to learn more. King Herod tricked the Wise Men. He told them: "Our prophets wrote that Christ would be born in Bethlehem. Look there for the Child, and when you have found Him, come and tell me, so that I may go to worship Him." King Herod lied. What he really planned to do was to kill the Infant King!

When the Wise Men left King Herod's palace, the star reappeared. They followed it to the place where the Holy Family was. After the Wise Men found Jesus, they planned to return to King Herod. However, an angel warned them not to see King Herod and to take a different way home.

When King Herod realized that the Wise Men would not return, he went into a rage. He ordered his soldiers to kill all the Jewish boy babies under the age of two. He thought that in this way, the Child King would be found and killed. It was a horrible, wicked crime!

Bless us, Mary, maiden mild;
Bless us, too, her tender Child.

1. When the Wise Men came to Jerusalem, the star _____.

2. Wicked King Herod planned to _____ Baby Jesus.

3. An _____ warned the Wise Men not to return to King Herod.

The Holy Family was still resting in Bethlehem. Joseph didn't know Baby Jesus was in danger. Then God sent an angel to St. Joseph. The angel came to Joseph in a dream. He told Joseph to wake up right away, take the Blessed Mother and Baby Jesus, and flee far away into the land of Egypt. Joseph quickly obeyed. They left that very night on their long trip. This journey is called the Flight into Egypt.

In their search for the Baby King, the evil soldiers killed all the boy babies they could find in Bethlehem. They killed many, many baby boys. On December 28, we remember the killing of the Holy Innocents. On that day, we recall all the poor babies killed by King Herod's cruel order.

Holy Innocents, pray for us.

1. An angel came to St. Joseph in a _____.

2. The angel told St. Joseph to flee to the land of _____.

3. We call the little babies killed by King Herod's soldiers the

   _____ _____.

Joseph took Mary and Jesus safely to Egypt. The Holy Family stayed there a long time waiting for an angel to tell them when they could go back to their own land and their own home. They had to wait until all danger had passed. This must have been very hard for the Holy Family. They had to live in an unknown country with no friends or relatives nearby. Mary and Joseph had to learn to speak the Egyptian language. St. Joseph had to find work to support the Holy Family. He did not know how long they would stay there. But St. Joseph was a holy man. He trusted in God. He worked and he prayed. Mary, too, worked and prayed very hard for her family.

St. Joseph was a carpenter. As the Child Jesus grew older, He helped St. Joseph in his shop. St. Joseph taught Him the skills of the carpenter's trade. Together they would make a plow, a chair, a table, or perhaps a baby's cradle. Jesus would sweep the sawdust from the floor. Jesus helped His mother as well. He helped her with the chores and helped her in the garden. He was always very good. When He played with other children, He never fought or became angry. He always treated other children kindly. He comforted those children who were teased by others and always included everyone in His company. Everyone loved Jesus. All the other children wanted to be good just like Jesus. What a wonderful example He was to the other children!

Let us follow the Child Jesus. Let us remember to help our parents with the many things they have to do. Be kind and patient with little brothers and sisters. Include others who may feel left out in your play. If we are obedient and kind and thoughtful like Our Lord, then our homes will be filled with love like the Holy Family's home.

Lord, make me an instrument of Thy peace.

1. St. Joseph was a _____.

2. Jesus always _____ His parents with their work.

3. We must try to _____ Our Lord's example.

Finally, the day came when King Herod died. An angel appeared again to St. Joseph in a dream. The angel told him that it was now safe to return to their own country. The Holy Family obeyed right away and returned to their home in Nazareth. Their house in Nazareth was simple. The Holy Family did not have much, but they were happy in their love for each other. The little house in Nazareth was a happy place where they prayed, worked, and played together.

Jesus was always ready to help His mother or His foster-father. He never disobeyed or talked back to them. Let us try to be good and kind like Jesus. Can you think of ways to follow the Child Jesus? Try to do your very best in your school lessons. Be neat in your work. Open your books the very first time you are told. Keep your room tidy. Help with the dishes or with sweeping the floors. Share your toys with your brothers and sisters. Be kind to everyone, even those who are not kind to you. In this way, you will help make your home a happy and holy place, like the home of Jesus in Nazareth.

Lovely Lady dressed in blue,
Teach me how to pray.
God was just your little Boy
And you know the way.

1. When _____ _____ died, it was safe for the Holy Family to return to their country.

2. The Holy Family lived in the town of _____.

3. I will make Jesus happy if I _____ Him.

Questions for Week Twelve

Day 1

1. Is St. Joseph the real father of Jesus?

   No, St. Joseph is the foster-father of Jesus. Christ's real Father is God the Father in Heaven.

2. Why did Herod want to kill Jesus?

   King Herod tried to kill Jesus because he thought Jesus was an Earthly king and would take away his throne and kingdom.

Day 2

1. What do we call the journey that the Holy Family made into Egypt?

   We call the journey the Flight into Egypt.

2. On what day do we remember the babies killed by King Herod?

   We honor them on the Feast of the Holy Innocents, December 28.

Day 3

1. What kind of work did St. Joseph do?

   St. Joseph was a carpenter.

2. Whom must all children imitate if they wish to be good?

   All children must imitate the Child Jesus if they wish to be good.

Day 4

How did the Holy Family know when to return to Nazareth?

An angel appeared to St. Joseph in a dream and told him they could return to Nazareth.

Jesus Begins His Public Life

When Jesus was twelve years old, the Holy Family went on a trip together with other families from Nazareth. They all were going to Jerusalem to pray in the Temple on a great holy day. Most traveled on foot; some rode on donkeys. On the way back home, Mary and Joseph realized that Jesus was not among the travelers.

In those days, the people traveled in separate groups: the men and older boys, the women and older girls. The families did not gather together until supper time. It was not until they had traveled back a full day that Mary and Joseph saw Jesus was not with the travelers. They quickly hurried back to Jerusalem to look for Jesus. They were worried, but they trusted in God. They knew Jesus is God. They searched for three days. Finally, they found Jesus in the Temple teaching the priests. The priests and the elders were amazed at His words and wondered, "How can a boy know so much about God?" The Boy Jesus knew so much more than any of them. They did not know that Jesus is God.

When Joseph and Mary found Jesus in the Temple, they asked Him why He had stayed behind. Jesus answered, "Do you not know that I must be about My Father's business?" Jesus was sent to Earth by God the Father. Jesus was teaching the learned men of the Temple about God His Father.

Jesus obediently went back to Nazareth with His mother Mary and St. Joseph. Jesus returned with them to the little home in Nazareth. He would not begin His mission until He was thirty years old. Then Jesus would leave His home to teach all people about God His Father.

Dear Jesus, grant that I may always do Your Will.

1. When Jesus was twelve, the Holy Family traveled to

   _____.

2. Jesus was missing for _____ days.

3. Jesus was _____ the learned men of the Temple about God.

66

While Jesus was growing up in Nazareth, His foster-father, St. Joseph, died. What a happy death St. Joseph must have had with Jesus and Mary at his side! That is why St. Joseph is known as the Patron of a Happy Death. Then Jesus took good care of His Mother Mary. He continued His foster-father's work as a carpenter.

When Jesus was thirty years old, it was time for Him to do the work of God His Father. He would teach the people about God and how to live. Most of all, He would redeem the world by suffering and dying on the Cross. That is how He would make up to God for the sins of people.

Jesus went to the River Jordan to see His cousin John, the son of St. Elizabeth. St. John was preaching penance to the people and baptizing them in the river. Our Lord went to His cousin and told John to baptize Him. John did not want to baptize Our Lord because he knew Jesus was the Son of God, the promised Savior. Jesus did not need to be baptized, but He wanted us to follow His example. We all need Baptism to wash away Original Sin. John obeyed Our Lord and baptized Him. Then a wonderful thing happened. The Bible tells us the heavens were opened, and the Holy Spirit, God, the Third Person of the Blessed Trinity, came down over the head of Our Lord in the form of a dove. The voice of God the Father said, "This is My beloved Son, in Whom I am well pleased." On this special day, the mystery of the Blessed Trinity was shown to us.

St. Joseph, Patron of a Happy Death, pray that I may die in the state of grace.

1. St. Joseph is the Patron of a Happy Death because he died with

_____ and _____ at his side.

2. Before He began His work, Jesus went to His cousin John to be

_____ in the River Jordan.

3. On the day of Our Lord's baptism, the mystery of the

_____ _____ was revealed to us.

After His baptism, Jesus went alone into the desert to fast and to pray. He did not eat for a very long time, forty days. He was weak and very hungry. The devil came to tempt Him. The devil thought he could tempt Jesus with food, with power, and with all the kingdoms of the world. Jesus commanded the devil to leave and said, "The Lord thy God shall you adore. Him alone shall you serve."

Jesus began to carry out His work to build His Church. His Church is the Catholic Church. Jesus chose twelve Apostles to help Him with His work. The word "Apostle" means one who is sent. These Apostles were close to Jesus and went everywhere He went. They left their homes to do the work Jesus called them to do. They went with Jesus from town to town and listened to Him as He taught the people about the Kingdom of God. At night, after the crowds went home, Jesus taught the Apostles more things about God and His Church.

Some of the Apostles were fishermen like Peter, James, and John. Matthew was a tax collector. They were all different, but they all loved Jesus. Jesus chose from the twelve a leader to lead His Church after He returned to Heaven. This leader was St. Peter. He was our first pope. He took the place of Christ on Earth. Jesus gave him special authority over His Church. There always has been a pope since the time of Peter. Many of them are saints. We must pray for our Holy Father, the pope, and thank God for him each day.

Our Lady, Queen of Apostles, pray for our Church.

1. Jesus went to the desert to _____ and to _____.

2. The word apostle means _____ who is _____.

3. The first pope was _____ _____.

Every day, Jesus taught crowds of people about God's love. He was often tired, but He always had time for the little children. He loved them to gather around Him. Our Lord told them about God's love and about His Father in Heaven. Jesus loves all children in a special way. He loves you very much, too. Our Lord Jesus said, "If you do not become like one of these little ones, you cannot enter the kingdom of Heaven."

One day, the Apostles saw Jesus praying to His Father. They said to Him, "Lord, teach us how to pray." Jesus then taught them a very special prayer. It is called the "Our Father":

Our Father, Who art in Heaven
Hallowed be Thy Name.
Thy Kingdom come,
Thy will be done
on Earth as it is in Heaven.
Give us this day our daily bread
and forgive us our trespasses
as we forgive those who trespass
against us.
And lead us not into temptation,
but deliver us from evil. Amen.

The "Our Father" was taught to us by Our Lord Himself! Therefore, it is the most important prayer. It is the perfect prayer. Make sure to say it with reverence each day, remembering that the words came straight from the lips of Jesus Christ, the Son of God.

1. Jesus loves little _____ in a special way.

2. Jesus gave us the prayer called the _____ _____.

3. The Our Father is the _____ prayer because it was taught to us by Jesus Christ Himself.

Questions for Week Thirteen

Day 1

1. Where did the Holy Family go when Our Lord Jesus was twelve years old?

   The Holy Family journeyed to the Temple in Jerusalem.

2. Where did Mary and Joseph find Jesus after He had been missing three days?

   Mary and Joseph found Jesus in the Temple explaining the Scriptures and teaching the learned men of the Temple about God His Father and the promised Savior.

3. Did Jesus obey His mother and foster-father?

   Yes, Jesus always obeyed His Mother Mary and St. Joseph, His foster-father.

Day 2

1. Why is St. Joseph the Patron of a Happy Death?

   St. Joseph is the Patron of a Happy Death because he died with Jesus and Mary at his side.

2. What do we call the men chosen by Jesus to be His closest followers?

   We call these men Apostles.

3. How many Apostles did Christ choose?

   Christ chose twelve men to be His Apostles.

Day 3

1. Whom did Jesus choose to be the head of the Apostles and of His Church?

    Jesus chose St. Peter to be the head of the Apostles and of His Church. St. Peter was the first pope.

2. Whose place does the current pope take?

    The pope takes the place of Our Lord Jesus Christ on Earth.

* 3. How does Jesus help all men to gain Heaven?

    Jesus helps all men to gain Heaven through the Catholic Church.

Day 4

Why do we call the Our Father the perfect prayer?

We call the Our Father the perfect prayer because it was given to us by Our Lord Jesus Christ, the Second Person of the Blessed Trinity.

The Miracles of Jesus

Jesus showed us that He is God in a very wonderful way. He worked miracles to show us that He is the Divine Son of God. When God does something different from the normal course of nature, that is, when something happens that is otherwise impossible, it is called a miracle. Jesus worked many miracles during His life on Earth. St. John, one of the Apostles and a writer of the Gospels, tells us that the world is not big enough to contain all the books needed to write about all the wonderful things Jesus has done.

Jesus worked His first public miracle at a wedding. Jesus and His Mother Mary went to a wedding feast in the town of Cana. Halfway through the celebration, the hosts ran out of wine. Mary knew the bridegroom would be embarrassed, so she told Jesus, "They have no wine." Then she told the servants, "Do whatever He tells you." Jesus told the servants to fill the empty wine jugs with water. Then He told them to take the jugs to the steward, the main servant. When the steward tasted what was in the jugs, he said to the groom, "Why, you have saved the best wine for last!" Jesus had turned the water into wine! This was the first public miracle of Our Lord that is in the Bible.

Our Lord's first public miracle tells us something very important. Jesus blesses weddings and people becoming married. He wants married people to obey His laws so they can be happy and, if they have children, so they can teach their children about God. At Cana, Jesus also shows us that we should care about our own mother's wishes. We must pray to Our Lady, the Blessed Mother Mary, because she asks Jesus to give us special favors. Mary can help us remember what Jesus wants us to do. Mary will help us come close to her Divine Son.

Mother of Divine Grace, bring our prayers to Jesus.

1. An action which no one can perform except God is called a

   _____.

2. Jesus worked His first public miracle at a _____ in Cana.

3. Jesus worked this miracle because His _____ asked Him to do so.

Crowds of people followed Our Lord wherever He went. They listened to everything He said. They asked Jesus to help them. They brought the sick and the crippled to Him to be healed.

One day, there was a great crowd of over five thousand men, besides all the women and children in the crowd. On a grassy hillside, they came to listen to Jesus speak. Our Lord preached all day, and the people grew hungry. Many of them had traveled long distances to see Him. The Apostles wanted to send them home, but Jesus knew they were too tired and hungry.

The Apostle Andrew found a boy who had brought five loaves of bread and two fish. But how could that feed so many? Jesus took the boy's food and blessed it. Then He told His Apostles to give the food to the people. Although there were thousands of people, there was plenty of food for everyone. After everyone had eaten, Jesus told the Apostles to gather up what was left. They gathered up twelve baskets full of bread and fish. This was one of Our Lord's greatest miracles. Jesus truly is the Son of God!

Jesus Christ, Son of God, have mercy on me.

1. St. Andrew found a boy who had five _____ of bread

   and two _____.

2. After everyone had their fill, _____ baskets of food were left over.

3. The multiplication of the loaves and fishes was one of Our Lord's

   greatest _____.

Jesus performed many different types of miracles. Once He was with the Apostles in a fishing boat on the Sea of Galilee. Jesus was sleeping in the boat. Suddenly, a dreadful storm came and tossed the little boat back and forth across the high waves. The Apostles were frightened for their lives, but still Jesus continued to sleep. The Apostles finally woke Him and said, "Save us, Lord, or we shall die!" Jesus calmly stood up in the boat and commanded the storm, "Stop!" Immediately, all was peaceful and still.

One time the Apostles were fishing from a boat, but this time Jesus was not with them. A dark and windy storm came across the lake, and the Apostles were terribly afraid. Peter looked out over the lake and couldn't believe what he saw! Jesus was walking toward him on the water! Jesus called out to Peter and told him to walk toward Our Lord on the water. Trusting in the power of Jesus, Peter climbed out of the boat and began walking on the water just like Jesus! But he soon lost confidence and grew frightened. At that moment, he began to sink. He cried out to Jesus, "Save me, Lord!" Jesus reached out and pulled him up out of the raging waves. Our Lord asked Peter, "Why did you lose faith!" Jesus wants us to have complete trust in Him. There is nothing for us to fear if we listen to Jesus and trust in Him.

Still another time, the Apostles had been out in the boat fishing all night long but had caught nothing. As the sun was coming up over the horizon early in the morning, they saw Jesus on the shore. He called them over and climbed into their boat. Jesus told them to go back into the deep water and lower their nets again. Peter was puzzled and said, "Master, we have been trying all night long, but we have no fish. Still, as You wish, I will try again." The nets were lowered once more. Immediately, the nets began to tug and jerk! The nets were full of fish! So full of fish were they that the nets began to break! This miracle teaches us a very important lesson: By ourselves we can do nothing. But with Jesus, we can do everything He wants us to do!

Most Sacred Heart of Jesus, I place my trust in Thee.

1. Jesus calmed the dreadful _____.

2. Jesus walked on the _____.

3. With Jesus, we can do _____ He wants us to do.

Jesus is truly God. He always answers our prayers.

Jesus had a very good friend, a young man named Lazarus who became very ill. Jesus was away preaching and was not there to help His friend. All through his sickness, the two sisters of Lazarus prayed for Jesus to come and heal their brother. But Jesus wanted to wait. He had another plan. Then Lazarus died. When Jesus was told about His friend's death, Jesus traveled to the home of Lazarus. When Jesus arrived, Lazarus had been dead four days and was already buried in the tomb. Jesus knew how hard the sisters of Lazarus had prayed. Jesus was sad they had lost their dear brother.

Martha, one of the sisters, said, "Lord, if You had been here, my brother would not have died." Jesus asked them to take Him to the tomb of Lazarus. When Jesus reached the tomb, everyone told Him it was too late. Then a wonderful thing happened! Suddenly, Jesus shouted: "Lazarus come forth!" To everyone's amazement, Lazarus walked out of his tomb! All were overjoyed at this miracle. The many friends of Lazarus ran back to the town of Bethany, yelling as they ran, "Lazarus is alive! Jesus brought him back from the dead!"

My Jesus, I love Thee with all my heart.

1. What was the name of the brother of Martha and Mary?

   _____

2. How long had their brother been dead when Jesus arrived?

   _____

3. _____ said, "Lord, if you had been here, my brother would not have died."

Questions for Week Fourteen

Day 1

1. Why did Jesus perform miracles?

   Jesus performed miracles to show that He is God.

2. Where did Jesus perform His first public miracle?

   Jesus performed His first public miracle at the wedding feast at Cana.

3. What miracle did Jesus perform at Cana?

   Jesus turned water into wine.

4. Who asked Jesus to perform this miracle?

   His Mother Mary asked Jesus to perform this miracle.

Day 2

1. How did Jesus feed the hungry crowd of five thousand men, besides women and children?

   Jesus miraculously increased five loaves of bread and two fishes to feed the entire crowd of more than five thousand people.

2. After everyone had their fill, how much food was left?

   After everyone had their fill, there were twelve baskets full of food left over.

Day 3

1. Why did Peter sink when he walked on the water?

   Peter sank because he allowed his fear to overcome his faith in Jesus.

2. What does Jesus show us by these miracles?

   Jesus shows us that He loves us and we must have complete faith in Him because He can do anything.

Day 4

1. How long was Lazarus dead before Jesus raised him back to life?

   Lazarus was dead in the tomb four days before Jesus raised him back to life.

* 2. Why did God the Son become man?

   God the Son became man to satisfy for the sins of all men and to help everybody to gain Heaven.

More Miracles and Parables of Our Lord

Jesus loves each one of us. He showed this by suffering and dying for us. He showed His love by curing many people of their illnesses. He also brought dead people back to life.

Once there was a Jewish official named Jairus whose young daughter was dying. Jairus walked several miles to find Jesus to ask Him to cure her. Before Jesus could walk back to his house, a servant met them and told Jairus it was too late. His daughter had died. Nevertheless, Jesus told Jairus to have faith and believe. They continued on their way to the home of Jairus. They entered the girl's room. The dead girl was surrounded by weeping relatives and friends. Jesus said, "Weep not! The girl is not dead, but only sleeping." The people saw the girl was dead, and laughed at Jesus. These people did not have faith in Jesus. Jairus made the people leave the room. Then Jesus took the little girl's hand and said, "Little girl, arise." Her soul returned to her body, and immediately she sat up. Her parents were astonished! Jesus told the parents to give her something to eat, because she was hungry. How thankful Jairus and his family were! Jesus wants us all to believe in Him the way Jairus did.

Another time, there was an important Roman soldier who also had great faith in Our Lord. The soldier had a sick servant whom he loved very much. He wanted Jesus to heal his servant, but the Roman soldier did not think he was good enough to have Jesus enter his home. He said to Jesus, "Lord, I am not worthy that You should come under my roof, but only say the word and my servant shall be healed." Jesus told the crowd He had not seen such faith in all of Israel. Our Lord told the Roman soldier to return home because his servant was cured.

Holy Mother Church uses the words of the Roman soldier at Mass to honor and remember to the end of time. At Holy Mass, when we adore Jesus in Holy Communion we say, "Lord, I am not worthy that You should enter under my roof, but only say the word, and my soul shall be healed." The Holy Eucharist is the way that God heals our souls.

Lord, I am not worthy that You should enter under my roof, but only say the word, and my soul shall be healed.

1. Jesus raised the daughter of _____ back to life.

2. The Roman soldier had greater _____ than many of the Chosen People.

3. We honor the Roman soldier's faith in God at every _____.

Certain groups of Jews were called Pharisees. Some Pharisees were among the teachers and experts in the Jewish religion. Many of the Pharisees did not like Jesus. They were jealous of Him and did not want to believe that He was the Savior sent by God.

One day, Jesus saw a crowd gathered around a blind man. The Pharisees and others were asking why the man was born blind.

Jesus told the crowd that the man was blind in order to show the glory of God. Then Jesus took some clay and rubbed it on the blind man's eyes. Jesus told him to wash in a certain pool of water. The blind man believed that Jesus is the Son of God. He quickly was led to the pool, where he washed his eyes. Suddenly, he could see! He ran back to Jesus and shouted: "I believe, Lord!" The blind man fell on his knees and adored Jesus. The man, cured of his lifelong blindness, thanked Jesus over and over again.

Lord, I believe! Help my unbelief.

1. Some _____ were among the teachers and experts in the Jewish religion.

2. The Pharisees did not want to believe that Jesus is the _____.

3. Jesus cured the man of his _____.

Jesus told stories to the crowds that followed Him. These were stories called parables that teach a lesson. With parables, Jesus taught us all how to live and act. The following parable is about the Good Samaritan.

Once there was a Jewish man who was traveling along the road. Suddenly, some robbers attacked him, stealing all his money and beating him. Badly beaten, the man was left on the road to die. A Jewish priest soon walked by, but he was in a hurry and did not stop to help the dying man. Later, a Levite came to the same place. A Levite was an important official in the Jewish temple. The Levite just looked at the dying man and went on his way. Finally, a Samaritan man came. The Samaritan people were looked down upon by the Jews.

When this Samaritan saw the dying man, he did not look upon him as an enemy. He was moved with pity. He stopped to help. He cleaned the Jewish man's wounds. He lifted the man and placed him on his own donkey and gave him his own coat to keep him warm. The Samaritan took the injured man to the nearest inn and paid the innkeeper to take good care of him. He told the innkeeper to do whatever was needed to make the man well again. If more money was required, the Samaritan told the innkeeper he would pay him when he returned.

After Jesus told this story, He asked, "Which man was a neighbor to the dying man?"

Do you know the answer? Christ wants us to treat everyone we meet as our neighbor. We must treat everyone the way we would want to be treated. Christ calls us to treat one another as He treated others.

Jesus Christ, Son of God, have mercy on me, a sinner!

1. Jesus told many special stories called _____.

2. The parable of the Good Samaritan shows that we must treat

   everyone as our _____.

Christ's miracles and parables are a special part of His message to us. Our Lord Jesus is God, and He loves each one of us very much. Miracles can be done only by the power of God. Our Lord's miracles proved that He is God. Through His miracles, Jesus showed His love for all people. His love teaches us how we must treat everyone. Miracles teach us to have faith in God.

Jesus told many parables because people could understand the lessons of these stories. Our Lord's parables are easy to understand and remember. His parables teach us how God wants us to live so that we can be happy with Him in Heaven. Christ told many more parables. We can read them in the Bible.

Lord, teach me Your ways.

1. Christ's miracles proved that He is _____.

2. Our Lord told parables to make the lessons easy to understand and _____.

3. We can find Our Lord's parables in the _____.

Questions for Week Fifteen

Day 1

What are the words of the Roman soldier that we pray at every Mass?

The words of the Roman soldier that we pray at every Mass are, "Lord, I am not worthy that You should enter under my roof, but only say the word, and my soul shall be healed."

Day 2

Why was the man born blind?

The man was born blind because his cure by Jesus would show the people that Jesus was the promised Redeemer. The miracle would give great honor and glory to God.

Day 3

1. What is a miracle?

   When God does something that is impossible for men to do and thus changes the course of nature, it is called a miracle.

2. What is a parable?

   A parable is a story that teaches an important lesson.

Day 4

Give two reasons why Jesus performed miracles.

Jesus performed miracles to show that He is God and to show that He loves and cares for all people.

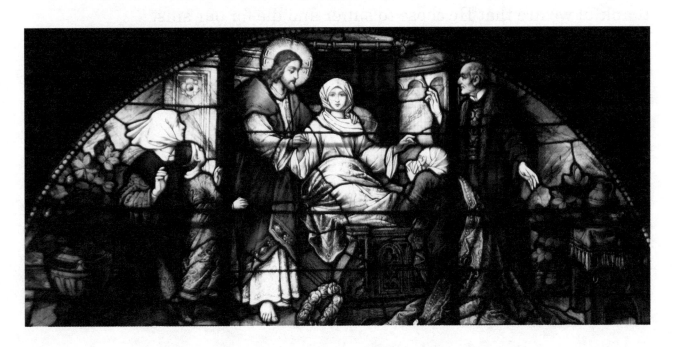

Holy Week:
Jesus Suffers and Dies for Our Sins

Lent is a special time of year when we remember the suffering and death of Jesus on the Cross. Lent lasts forty days. It begins on Ash Wednesday, a special day of prayer and penance. On Ash Wednesday, the priest uses ashes to mark our foreheads with the Sign of the Cross. He says to each person who receives the ashes, "Remember, you are dust, and to dust you will return." This is to remind us that someday our bodies will die.

During Lent, we prepare ourselves for Good Friday. We pray, fast, and make special acts of self-denial or sacrifice. We deny ourselves things that we like. We do this to show God how much we love Him. We should give up some pleasures during Lent. In this way, we can imitate Our Lord's sufferings and have a share in them as well.

Can you think of ways to make sacrifices during this holy season? We can do without a snack, a candy bar, or a television show. We can save up our snack money and put it in the poor box in church. We should try to perform more good works than we usually do.

We should make an extra effort to help in our home. We should obey our parents right away. We should be extra kind to our brothers and sisters. We should make a special effort to attend Mass each day during Lent. We should say special prayers to Jesus. We should tell Him how thankful we are that He chose to suffer and die for our sins.

O my Jesus,
it is for love of Thee that I make this offering.

1. Lent is the time of year when the Church remembers Our Lord's
   _____ and _____ on the Cross.

2. During Lent we prepare ourselves by prayer, fasting, and special acts of _____.

Jesus is God and the Second Person of the Blessed Trinity. He knows all things. Jesus knew when the time of His death was near. After teaching the people and working many miracles for three years, He was about to do His greatest work. He was about to offer Himself as a sacrifice to God for us. On Holy Thursday, the night before Our Lord's death, Jesus left a special gift for His Apostles and for everyone in His Church. Jesus called His Apostles together in the Upper Room for their last meal together. This special meal is called the Last Supper because it would be their last time together before the death of Our Lord.

A very holy moment came. Jesus took bread and blessed it. He broke the bread, saying, "Take and eat. This is My Body." Then He gave It to His Apostles. Next, Jesus took a cup of wine, blessed it, and said, "This is the cup of My Blood. Do this in remembrance of Me."

At that holy moment, when Jesus said those sacred words, the bread and wine no longer were bread and wine. They became Our Lord's Body and Blood, Soul and Divinity. Jesus had just said the first Mass. The Apostles received Jesus in the first Holy Communion. This was the great gift of Jesus to His Church.

When Jesus said, "Do this in remembrance of Me," He made the Apostles His first priests and bishops. He gave them the power to change bread and wine into His Body and Blood. The Apostles were given the power to offer Our Lord's Sacrifice, the Mass.

His love for us is so great that Jesus did not want to leave us without Himself, even though He had to return to Heaven. He used this way to remain with us until the end of the world. He gave us Himself in the Holy Eucharist. He gave us priests and bishops to be sure there would always be the Mass and the Blessed Sacrament. Can we ever know how much love God has for us?

Jesus, my Lord, my God, my All,
how can I love Thee as I ought?

1. Jesus taught the people and worked miracles for _____ years.

2. On _____ _____ Jesus gave a great gift to the Apostles and to all of us.

3. Jesus is truly present in the _____ _____.

After the Last Supper, Jesus took three of His Apostles, Peter, James, and John, to pray with Him in the Garden of Gethsemane. Jesus was preparing for the terrible suffering and death He was about to endure. He prayed very hard all night. He prayed and suffered so much that He began to sweat blood. His Apostles had fallen asleep. Jesus saw all the sins of everyone in the world, from Adam's first sin, down to the sin of the last person on Earth. It hurt Jesus to see all the sin in the world. Each time we are tempted to sin, let us remember Jesus suffering in the Garden.

Late that night, the soldiers marched into the Garden to arrest Jesus. They came with clubs and swords, ropes and chains for our gentle Lord. Judas, one of the twelve Apostles, showed the soldiers Who Jesus was by giving Jesus a kiss. Judas was paid thirty pieces of silver to betray Our Lord and God. This was a terrible, terrible sin. The other Apostles were frightened and ran out of the Garden. They hid from the soldiers and left Jesus alone with His enemies. His own friends had deserted Him.

My loving Jesus,
I am sorry for the sufferings my sins have given You.

1. After the Last Supper, Jesus went into the Garden of

   Gethsemane to _____.

2. While Jesus prayed and suffered, the Apostles had fallen

   _____.

3. Judas betrayed Jesus with a _____.

The leaders of the Jewish people wanted Jesus killed. They brought Jesus to Pontius Pilate, the Roman governor. Pilate was not a bad man, but he was not a strong man. He was a coward. He knew Jesus had done nothing wrong. Pilate asked Our Lord, "Are You the King of the Jews?" Jesus answered, "I am a King, but My Kingdom is not of this world." Our Lord's words worried Pilate. He said to the men who had brought Jesus to him, "This Man has done nothing wrong." The enemies of Our Lord only grew more angry.

Pilate thought he could find a way to save Jesus and not worry about the Jews. Each year on the feast of the Passover, Pilate set a prisoner free. He remembered the criminal Barabbas. Barabbas was a murderer. Surely, the people would want Jesus released and not Barabbas. Pilate put Barabbas and Jesus together on a balcony for the people to choose. "Whom do you wish me to free?" Pilate asked the crowd. "Give us Barabbas! Give us Barabbas!" they shouted. Pilate then asked, "What do you want me to do with Jesus?" The wicked crowd yelled back, "Crucify Him! Crucify Him!" Pilate could not believe his ears. "Why? What evil has this Man done?" But the crowd shouted all the more, "Crucify Him!"

With this, Pilate washed his hands in front of the crowd while he said, "The blood of this innocent Man is not on my hands. It is on yours." Pilate knew Jesus had done no wrong. Yet, because he was a coward, Pilate permitted Jesus to be killed.

Jesus, meek and uncomplaining, help me to bear wrongs patiently.

1. The Jews brought Jesus to the Roman governor, _____ _____.

2. Pilate knew that Jesus was an _____ Man.

3. When the crowd chose Barabbas, Pilate _____ his hands.

Questions for Week Sixteen

Day 1

1. Why does the priest put ashes on our foreheads on Ash Wednesday?
   The priest puts ashes on our foreheads to remind us that someday our bodies will die.

2. How should we prepare ourselves during the holy season of Lent?
   During Lent, we prepare ourselves by prayer, fasting, and making special acts of self-denial.

Day 2

What special and lasting gift did Jesus give the Apostles and the Church at the Last Supper?
   Jesus gave us the Holy Sacrifice of the Mass and Himself in the Holy Eucharist, the Blessed Sacrament, in order to be with us until the end of the world.

Day 3

Why did Jesus suffer so terribly in the Garden of Gethsemane?
   Jesus suffered greatly for two reasons:

   1) He knew the suffering and death He would soon undergo.

   2) He saw the sins of every person who had ever lived and who would live until the end of the world.

Day 4

Did Pilate wish to condemn Jesus to death?
   No, Pilate saw that Jesus was an innocent Man. Pilate was a coward and condemned Jesus to death because he feared the Jews.

The Stations of the Cross

During Lent, there are special prayers we can say each day to remember Our Lord's sufferings. These special prayers are called the Stations of the Cross. Each one shows a part of Our Lord's sufferings on the Way to Calvary as He carried His Cross. They help us to think about the sufferings Jesus went through before He died.

We find the Stations of the Cross along the walls of every Roman Catholic church. There are fourteen Stations of the Cross. Walk to each Station and stop to pray. Before each one, genuflect, and say this prayer:

We adore Thee, O Christ, and we bless Thee,
Because by Thy holy Cross,
Thou hast redeemed the world.

✟ The First Station: Jesus Is Condemned to Death

Pilate tells Jesus He must die on the Cross. Jesus does not complain. He knows this pleases God His Father. We, too, must not complain about things we do not want to do. We want to please God the Father like Jesus did. This is how we unite with Jesus on the Cross.

✟ The Second Station: Jesus Takes up His Cross

Jesus is already weak and exhausted from the beating by the soldiers. Somehow, He struggles and picks up His Cross. No matter how tired we may be, or how unpleasant something may be for us, we must overcome ourselves and do what Our Lord expects of us. In this way, we walk with Jesus up the hill to Calvary.

The special prayers that remind us of Our Lord's sufferings are the Stations of the _____.

✠ The Third Station: Jesus Falls the First Time

The Cross is so heavy, and Jesus is so weak, that He falls to the ground while carrying the Cross. But He rises from the ground and keeps on going. Jesus shows us that even when we sin we must try again to be good and keep going toward Heaven. Each time we sin, we hurt Jesus, because it is our sins that made Him fall.

✠ The Fourth Station: Jesus Meets His Mother

Jesus sees His Mother as He struggles up the hill. Mary knows Jesus is suffering for our sins. Jesus knows His Mother is suffering to see Him. She does not run away like the Apostles, but stays to be at her Son's side. We can comfort Jesus, too, by helping others who need us. Mary is by our side as our loving Mother. We should ask her help to keep us from sin. She will always be with us, no matter how hard the way may be.

✠ The Fifth Station: Simon Helps Jesus Carry His Cross

Jesus becomes very weak. The soldiers are afraid that He will die before making it to the top of the hill. They force a man from Cyrene, named Simon, to help Jesus carry His Cross. Jesus gives Simon one glance that shows His gratitude for his kindness. Our Lord's glance fills Simon's heart. He willingly carries the Cross for Jesus. The more good works we do, the more special gifts of grace Jesus gives us.

✠ The Sixth Station: Veronica Wipes the Face of Jesus

In the crowd is a lady named Veronica. When she sees the bloodied, dirty face of Jesus, she is filled with pity. The soldiers are threatening, and the crowd is wild, but Veronica does not care. She does what is right. She steps out of the crowd and tenderly wipes Our Lord's face with her veil. Jesus is so grateful that He leaves her a wonderful gift: the image of His Holy Face on the cloth. Like Veronica, we too must step out of the crowd to do what is right. We must always do what is right, even if we see others disobey God's Law. God will reward us with His graces, and with eternal happiness with Him in Heaven.

✝ The Seventh Station: Jesus Falls the Second Time

Jesus again falls to the ground with the weight of our sins heavy upon His shoulders. Again, He gets up. Jesus shows us that even though we fall into sin over and over, we must ask forgiveness each time and try again, no matter how difficult it is. We must continue to do what God wants.

✝ The Eighth Station: Jesus Speaks to the Holy Women

Jesus meets a group of holy women along the way. They are crying because they know Jesus does not deserve this horrible treatment. Jesus tells them not to cry for Him, but for themselves and their children.

✝ The Ninth Station: Jesus Falls the Third Time

Once again, Jesus falls on the road to Calvary. This time He is so worn out from loss of blood and His terrible pain, that it would be easy to just stay on the ground. Instead, Jesus uses all His remaining strength, forces Himself to stand once more, and continues. We must remember Our Lord's loving goodness, and quickly rise from the ugliness of sin.

✝ The Tenth Station: Jesus Is Stripped of His Garments

Jesus finally reaches the top of Calvary where He is to be nailed to the Cross. He is ready to finish the work His Heavenly Father gave Him. The soldiers now start to tear off His clothes. Their harshness rips open His wounds again. Jesus does not utter a word of complaint. We must ask Jesus to strip away anything that keeps us away from Him.

✝ The Eleventh Station: Jesus Is Nailed to the Cross

The soldiers are very rough with Jesus. They throw Him down on the Cross. With a heavy blow of the hammer, a nail is driven right through His feet and then two others into His hands. Jesus is in unspeakable pain, but He still does not complain. Let us remember all that Jesus had to suffer and offer up our little aches and pains without complaint.

✝ The Twelfth Station: Jesus Dies on the Cross

Jesus does not die on the Cross right away, but hangs in agony for three long hours. He forgives His enemies and gives Himself to His Father to atone, or make up, for our sins. He tells St. John that Mary is now his Mother, too. When Jesus says this, He is also giving His Mother to each one of us. Mary should mean to us what she meant to Jesus. Let us go to Jesus through Mary. After Jesus gives His Mother to the world, He says a prayer to His Heavenly Father, "Father, into Thy hands I commend My spirit." Jesus dies.

✝ The Thirteenth Station: Jesus Is Taken Down from the Cross

Joseph of Arimathea is a friend of Jesus. Joseph takes the Body of Jesus down from the Cross. Mary, His Mother, is also there. She holds Jesus in her arms and sees how badly He has been beaten. She looks at His Face, once so beautiful. Her own heart is pierced with a sword of sorrow as she looks upon His lifeless Body. She wants to help us not to sin. Our Blessed Mother wants us to ask her for help. Jesus gave her to us to help us be good.

✝ The Fourteenth Station: Jesus Is Laid in the Tomb

Some holy women who are friends of Jesus and Mary come to prepare Our Lord's Body for His burial. They weep when they look at Him. Our Lady feels this final separation greatly, especially when the tomb is sealed. With all our hearts, we must ask Our Lady always to keep us close to Jesus, and never let anything separate us from His love.

Did you know that the Church gives many special blessings, called indulgences, each time we pray the Stations of the Cross? It is good to say the Stations of the Cross often, particularly on Fridays, and especially in Lent.

Holy Mother pierce me through,
In my heart each wound renew
Of my Savior Crucified.

1. There are _____ Stations of the Cross.

2. We should say the Stations often, particularly on Fridays, and

    especially during _____.

Questions for Week Seventeen

Day 1

1. On what should we meditate when we say the Stations of the Cross?
   When we say the Stations of the Cross we should meditate on the suffering and death of Our Lord Jesus Christ.

2. How many Stations of the Cross are there?
   There are fourteen Stations of the Cross.

* 3. How did Jesus satisfy for the sins of all men?
   Jesus satisfied for the sins of all men by His sufferings and death on the Cross.

Day 2

1. How many times did Jesus fall on the Way of the Cross?
   Jesus fell three times on the Way of the Cross.

2. Who helped Jesus carry His cross?
   Simon of Cyrene helped Jesus carry His Cross.

3. Who stepped out of the crowd to wipe Our Lord's face?
   Veronica stepped out of the crowd to wipe Our Lord's face, and in gratitude Our Lord left the imprint of His Sacred Face on her veil.

Day 3

What did Jesus tell the holy women of Jerusalem?
   Jesus told the holy women to weep not for Him, but for themselves and for their children.

Day 4

1. Whom did Jesus give to us from the Cross?
   From the Cross, Jesus gave us His own Mother Mary.

2. Where can we find the Stations of the Cross?
   We can find the Stations of the Cross on the walls of every Catholic church.

Second Quarter Review

WEEK EIGHTEEN: Day 1   Review work from Weeks 10, 11, and 12

WEEK EIGHTEEN: Day 2   Review work from Weeks 13, 14, and 15

WEEK EIGHTEEN: Day 3   Review work from Weeks 16 and 17

WEEK EIGHTEEN: Day 4   Take Second Quarter Test

Note: If extra time is needed for review, use Day 4 to review. Use Day 5 to take the test.

Third Quarter

The Resurrection and Ascension of Our Lord

Our Lord's Body was placed in the tomb late Good Friday afternoon. Pilate placed soldiers in front of His tomb to be sure no one stole the Body of Jesus. Early Easter Sunday morning, according to the Gospel of Matthew, chapter 28, there was a great earth quake, and "an angel from the Lord descended from Heaven, and coming, rolled back the stone, and sat upon it. His countenance [face] was [as bright] as lightning and his raiment [clothes] [as bright] a snow. And for fear of him, [the angel], the guards were struck with terror and became as dead men." The soldiers seemed to faint in fear!

Mary Magdalen and some of the other holy women came to the tomb that morning. The tomb was empty! An angel sat inside the tomb. The angel told them, "Jesus is not here. He has risen!" How happy they were! Jesus was alive! The angel told them to hurry and tell the Apostles the good news.

When the Apostles heard the news that Jesus had risen from the dead, Peter and John ran to the grave to see if it were true. When they found only a folded linen cloth in the tomb, they said, "Truly, Jesus is God! He is risen as He said He would!"

Later that day, Jesus suddenly appeared to the Apostles in the Upper Room. Jesus smiled and held out His hands and showed them His feet. The wounds from the nails were still there. He said, "Peace be to you! It is I! Do not be afraid!" Joy filled their hearts, tears filled their eyes, and they fell to their knees. Truly, Jesus is the Son of God!

O good Jesus, within Thy wounds, hide me.

1. Soldiers were placed outside the tomb to be sure no one

   _____ Our Lord's Body.

2. Two of the Apostles, _____ and _____, ran to the tomb.

3. Jesus appeared to the Apostles and showed them the marks of

   the nails in His _____.

One of the Apostles, Thomas, was not in the Upper Room when Jesus came. When Thomas returned, he would not believe the other Apostles' story. He would not believe that Jesus had risen from the dead. He would not believe that Jesus had appeared to them. He said, "Unless I place my fingers into the wounds of His hands and in His side, I will not believe!"

Then Jesus came to the Apostles another day. This time, Thomas was with them. Jesus went to Thomas and showed His hands and side. When Thomas saw Our Lord's wounds, he was ashamed that he had not believed. He dropped to his knees and exclaimed, "My Lord and my God!"

Jesus then said something very important: "Now that you have seen Me, Thomas, you believe. Blessed are those who have not seen Me, yet believe." Jesus means us! We have not seen Jesus, but we know He is here. We know He is in our Church and in the Blessed Sacrament. We know He comes into our hearts when we receive Him in Holy Communion. We know that He has died and has risen from the dead. Alleluia!

When Jesus Christ appeared to the Apostles after His Resurrection, His Body had changed. His Body was glorified. He did things that He did not do before. With His glorified Body, Jesus walked through solid walls and doors. He instantly appeared and disappeared.

Jesus told us that our bodies, too, will rise from the dead at the Last Judgment. If we have been good, our bodies will be glorified also. Our bodies will be reunited to our souls at the end of the world. If we have been good, our bodies and souls will be happy with Jesus forever in Heaven. We must remember this throughout our Earthly lives if we want to spend eternity with God.

My Lord and my God!

1. Thomas the Apostle did not believe that Jesus had _____.

2. After His resurrection, Our Lord's Body was _____.

3. At the Last Judgment, our bodies will rise and be

    _____ to our souls.

Jesus Christ stayed on Earth for forty days after He had risen from the dead. During that time Jesus prepared the Apostles so they could continue the work He had begun. Then they understood why He had suffered, died, and risen from the dead. They understood what He meant by His Kingdom. His Kingdom is the Holy Catholic Church, and they were to be the first bishops. During the forty days, Jesus appeared and disappeared. This made the Apostles strong in their faith. They knew that Jesus was with them, even when they could not see Him.

One day, Jesus appeared to His Apostles after they had been fishing. He prepared a meal for them and ate with them. Jesus asked Peter three times, "Do you love Me?" Peter answered, "Yes, Lord, you know all things. You know I love You." Jesus told him, "Feed My sheep. Feed My lambs." Jesus was telling Peter He wanted him to be the head of Our Lord's Church on Earth. After Our Lord went back to Heaven, Peter would be the pope and take care of us, Our Lord's flock of sheep and lambs. Jesus was reminding Peter and the other Apostles of what He had told them before. Jesus named Peter the "Rock" on which He was going to build His Church, and gave Peter the keys to the Kingdom of Heaven. Peter takes the place of Jesus in His Church on Earth. Every pope who follows also takes the place of Jesus.

Peter is now a saint in Heaven. Our present Holy Father continues Peter's work and watches over Our Lord's flock with the same loving care. Jesus speaks to us, His flock, through the Holy Father, the pope, the head of the Catholic Church on Earth.

Dearest Lord, protect our Holy Father, the pope.

1. After He had risen from the dead, Jesus returned and stayed on

   Earth _____ days.

2. Our Lord's Kingdom on Earth is the _____ Church.

3. Jesus made Peter the head of His Church, the first _____.

Finally, the time came for Jesus to return to His Father in Heaven. The Apostles, Jesus' Mother Mary, and other disciples of Our Lord followed Jesus to a place called Mount Olivet. They climbed to the top of the mountain. Then Jesus told them His work on Earth was complete. He reminded them one last time, "Go and teach all nations, baptizing them in the Name of the Father, and of the Son, and of the Holy Spirit." He wanted every person in the world to know about Him and His teachings. Because God loves everyone, He wants everyone to know, love, and serve Him, and be happy with Him forever in Heaven.

Jesus blessed the crowd and slowly began to rise from the ground. He soon disappeared in the clouds while the Apostles silently watched. Two angels then appeared to the crowd and said, "Why do you stand looking up into Heaven? This Jesus, Who has returned to Heaven, will come back in the same way as you have seen Him going up into Heaven."

We call this day Ascension Thursday. On that day, forty days after Our Lord's Resurrection from the dead, Jesus returned to Heaven.

Lord Jesus Christ, Thou alone art holy,
Thou alone art Lord, Thou alone art the Most High.

1. Jesus told the Apostles, "Go and teach _____ _____ all nations."

2. Jesus returned to Heaven _____ days after His Resurrection.

Questions for Week Nineteen

Day 1

* 1. When was Our Lord's body placed in the tomb?

     Our Lord's body was placed in the tomb on Good Friday.

* 2. Who was the holy woman who came to the tomb on Sunday morning?

     Mary Magdalen was one of the holy women who came to the tomb on Sunday morning.

  3. Who were the two Apostles who ran to the grave?

     Peter and John were the two Apostles who ran to the grave.

Day 2

  1. What did Jesus tell the Apostle Thomas, who would not believe He had risen?

     Jesus said, "Blessed are those who have not seen Me, yet believe."

  2. What did St. Thomas say when He saw the risen Christ?

     St. Thomas dropped to his knees and said, "My Lord and my God!"

Day 3

* 1. How does Jesus help all men to gain Heaven?

     Jesus helps all men to gain Heaven through the Catholic Church.

  2. Who was the first pope of Our Lord's Catholic Church?

     St. Peter was the first pope of Our Lord's Catholic Church.

Day 4

  1. From what place did Christ ascend into Heaven?

     Christ ascended into Heaven from Mount Olivet.

  2. Who witnessed Our Lord's Ascension into Heaven?

     The Apostles, the Blessed Mother, and other disciples of Jesus witnessed His Ascension into Heaven.

Pentecost: The Birthday of the Church

After Jesus ascended into Heaven, the Apostles and the Blessed Mother returned to the Upper Room where Jesus had instituted the Holy Eucharist at the Last Supper. Earnestly they prayed, waiting for something very wonderful to happen. Before Jesus left, He told them that they would not be alone. Jesus said He would send the Holy Spirit to fill them with courage. The Holy Spirit would enlighten their minds to teach everyone in the world about Him and His Church.

Do you remember Who the Holy Spirit is? The Holy Spirit is God, the Third Person of the Blessed Trinity.

Come, Holy Spirit, fill the hearts of Thy faithful.

1. After the Ascension, the Apostles and Our Lady returned to the

   Upper Room to _____.

2. Jesus told them they would not be _____.

3. The Holy Spirit is God, the _____ _____ of
   the Blessed Trinity.

The Apostles and the Blessed Virgin Mary waited and prayed for the Holy Spirit in the Upper Room for nine days. It must have been a big comfort for the Apostles to have the Blessed Mother with them. The Apostles were frightened. They thought that the enemies of Jesus would come and kill them, too. They stayed in the Upper Room praying and preparing for the coming of the Holy Spirit.

On the tenth day, the Holy Spirit came. "And suddenly there came a sound from Heaven, as of a mighty wind coming, and it filled the whole house where they were sitting" (Acts of the Apostles 2:2). Suddenly, tongues of fire appeared above the heads of everyone in the room. That is how the Holy Spirit appeared. The fire showed the deep love of Christ which would burn inside the Apostles forever. They were on fire with love for Jesus. The fears they had known before disappeared. The Apostles were brave now. They were ready to face Our Lord's enemies and any other dangers that would come their way. They were ready to live and die to spread the Good News about Jesus. The Holy Spirit had transformed them into the first soldiers in the army of Christ.

The Apostles praised and thanked God. The fire of the Holy Spirit made them remember and understand everything that Jesus had taught them so they could go and tell others.

Come, Holy Ghost, Creator blest,
And in our hearts take up Thy rest.

1. The Apostles and Our Lady prayed for _____ days.

2. The Holy Spirit came in the form of tongues of _____.

3. The Holy Spirit transformed the Apostles into brave

   _____ in Christ's army.

The miraculous day on which the Holy Spirit came in the form of tongues of fire upon the Apostles and Our Lady is called Pentecost. Pentecost took place ten days after the Ascension of Our Lord Jesus into Heaven. Many wonderful things happened that day. The Holy Spirit gave the Apostles special miraculous gifts.

After the Holy Spirit descended on the Apostles, St. Peter instantly became very brave. He walked out of the Upper Room onto a balcony and preached to all the people in the streets below. There were crowds of people in Jerusalem that day. Travelers from different countries had come to Jerusalem to celebrate a religious holiday. An amazing thing happened: everyone in the streets heard St. Peter in his own country's language! People had come from places such as Rome, Greece, Egypt, Syria, and Africa. Even though St. Peter and the Apostles spoke in their own language, all were able to understand them! Three thousand men were baptized that day, as well as many women and children.

God gave them this gift so that they could go to the different nations and the people would understand them as they taught about Jesus as well as God the Father and God the Holy Spirit.

Send forth Thy Spirit and they shall be created, and Thou shalt renew the face of the Earth.

1. The day the Holy Spirit came upon the Apostles and Our Lady is

   called _____.

2. People from different countries were able to understand St. Peter

   and the Apostles in their own _____.

3. Peter walked outside of the _____ _____ to preach from the balcony.

The day on which God the Holy Spirit came to the Apostles is called Pentecost Sunday. It also is called the birthday of the Church. On this day, the Catholic Church that Jesus Christ started came to life. Jesus sent God the Holy Spirit to be with the Church right from its beginning. God the Holy Spirit guards and guides the Catholic Church in truth, and will do so until the end of the world. That is why the Catholic Church will last until the end of the world. The Holy Spirit keeps Our Lord's Church holy and alive, now and always!

Holy Spirit, come with Thy grace and heavenly aid, To fill the hearts which Thou hast made.

1. Pentecost also is called the _____ of the Church.

2. God the Holy Spirit has been with the Catholic Church right from

   its _____.

3. God the Holy Spirit guards and _____ the Catholic Church in God's truth.

Questions for Week Twenty

Day 1

Who is the Holy Spirit?

The Holy Spirit is God, the Third Person of the Blessed Trinity.

Day 2

1. How many days did the Apostles wait for the Holy Spirit after the Ascension?

   The Apostles waited nine days for the Holy Spirit.

2. In what form did the Holy Spirit come?

   The Holy Spirit came in the form of tongues of fire, resting on the heads of the Apostles and Our Lady.

Day 3

1. What do we call the day on which the Holy Spirit came?

   We call the day on which the Holy Spirit came Pentecost Sunday.

2. How many people did the Apostles baptize on Pentecost Sunday?

   On Pentecost Sunday, the Apostles baptized over three thousand men, not counting the women and children who were baptized.

Day 4

1. Why is Pentecost Sunday called the birthday of the Church?

   Pentecost Sunday is called the birthday of the Church because it is on that day that the Catholic Church came to life.

2. Did Jesus Christ start a Church?

   Yes, Jesus Christ started the Catholic Church.

The Sacraments and the Life of Grace

Jesus Christ started the Catholic Church so that we would know what to do in order to go to Heaven. The Apostles and disciples were the first bishops and priests of the Catholic Church. Our bishops and priests today act in the same way as the Apostles did. They are our teachers and friends. They help us to know Jesus and show us the way to Heaven.

We can go to Heaven only if we have the life of grace within us. Grace is God's own life in our souls. Grace makes us happy to do God's Will. Grace makes us strong to resist sin when we are tempted. Grace makes us pure. Grace makes us want to be like Jesus. The more grace we have, the happier and closer we will be to Jesus.

Mary, Mother of Divine Grace, help us be holy and pleasing to Jesus.

1. Jesus started the Catholic Church to show us what to do in order

   to go to _____.

2. The Apostles and disciples were the first _____

   and _____ of the Catholic Church.

3. We can go to Heaven only if we have the life of

   _____ within us.

Jesus Christ gave His Church seven important ways in which we gain His life of grace in our souls. These seven ways are called sacraments. They were given to us by Jesus Christ to give us grace. A sacrament gives us God's life of grace. Jesus Himself gives us the sacraments through His bishops and priests.

The seven sacraments are the very heart of the Church. We enter the Church by receiving the Sacrament of Baptism soon after we are born. We continue to receive the sacraments until we die.

Can you name the seven sacraments? They are Baptism, Penance or Reconciliation, Holy Eucharist, Confirmation, Holy Orders, Matrimony, and Anointing of the Sick. Anointing of the Sick is also known as Extreme Unction. We will learn all about them in the next few chapters.

O Holy Spirit, sweet Guest of my soul, abide in me and grant that I may ever abide in Thee.

1. Jesus gave us _____ important ways to gain His life of grace.

2. These important ways are called _____.

3. Jesus Himself gives us the sacraments through His _____

   and _____.

Can you name the first sacrament that you received? We receive the Holy Spirit for the first time when we receive the Sacrament of Baptism. Jesus promised the Apostles that the Holy Spirit would be with the Catholic Church always. The Holy Spirit can be with us always, too, after we receive Him in grace at Baptism.

The Sacrament of Baptism brings many wonderful gifts to us. Baptism makes us official members of the Catholic Church. Without Baptism, we could not receive any of the other wonderful sacraments of the Church.

The most important reason why Jesus gave us the Sacrament of Baptism is to remove Original Sin. Do you remember what happened when Adam and Eve sinned? They lost the life of grace in their souls for themselves and for their children, the whole human race. Their sin was the first sin, and is called Original Sin. We have all inherited Original Sin from our first parents, Adam and Eve. We are all born with Original Sin on our souls. Only the Sacrament of Baptism can take away Original Sin and make us members of the Church.

The sevenfold gifts of grace are Thine, O Finger of the hand Divine.

1. _____ is the first sacrament that we receive.

2. On our Baptism day, we receive the _____

    _____ for the first time.

3. Baptism takes away _____ _____ from our souls.

When we are baptized, Original Sin is removed from our souls. God gives us His Sanctifying Grace for the first time. When we receive Sanctifying Grace at Baptism, our bodies and souls become temples of the Holy Spirit. We become a special child of God. God lives within us. We become holy and pleasing to God. We become members of the Catholic Church.

We are born into the world with the stain of Original Sin which we inherit from Adam and Eve. At Baptism, Original Sin is removed from our souls, and we are born into the Church. God gives us many wonderful gifts. He gives us His Holy Spirit. The Holy Spirit helps us to love God more and love all people. The Holy Spirit gives us the special gifts of Faith, Hope, and Charity.

Let us remember that our souls are pure and free of sin at Baptism, and we should try to keep them that way. Although Baptism takes away the stain of Original Sin, we still have a strong inclination toward sin.

We must be very careful not to sin. Ask God for special help to keep Him in your heart.

Holy Spirit, Thy grace and mercy send, Grant salvation in the end.

1. Baptism removes Original Sin, and our bodies and souls become

   temples of the _____ _____.

2. We must be very careful not to _____.

Questions for Week Twenty-one

Day 1:

1. Who were the first bishops and priests of the Catholic Church?
   The Apostles and disciples were the first bishops and priests of the Catholic Church.

* 2. What is grace?
   Grace is God's own life in my soul.

Day 2:

* 1. How does the Catholic Church help us to gain Heaven?
   The Catholic Church helps us to gain Heaven through the sacraments.

* 2. What is a sacrament?
   A sacrament is an outward sign, instituted by Christ to give grace.

* 3. What does grace do to the soul?
   Grace makes the soul holy and pleasing to God.

Day 3:

* 1. What sacrament did you receive as a baby?
   I received the Sacrament of Baptism.

* 2. What did Baptism do for you?
   Baptism washed away Original Sin from my soul and made it rich in the grace of God.

Day 4:

1. After Baptism, do our bodies become temples of the Holy Spirit?
   Yes, after Baptism our bodies become temples of the Holy Spirit.

2. What are the three special gifts that we receive at Baptism?
   The three special gifts we receive at Baptism are faith, hope, and charity.

3. After Baptism, do we still have a strong inclination to sin?
   Yes, after Baptism, we still have a strong inclination to sin even though Original Sin has been removed.

The Sacrament of Penance

When we receive the Sacrament of Baptism, we are filled with Sanctifying Grace. Even so, sometimes we sin and offend God. We lose God's grace within us when we commit a serious sin, a mortal sin. Our loving Jesus has given us a special gift to regain His grace. It is called the Sacrament of Penance. In the Sacrament of Penance, we tell God that we are sorry for our sins, and He gives us His forgiveness through the words of the priest. God will forgive us if we are truly sorry, no matter how bad our sin is. God forgives us because He loves us so much.

Jesus gave the Apostles the Sacrament of Penance on the day He rose from the dead. When Jesus appeared to the Apostles in the Upper Room, He said, "Whose sins you shall forgive, they are forgiven them. Whose sins you shall retain, they are retained." With these words, Jesus Christ gave the Apostles the power to forgive sins in His Name. The Apostles passed this power along to others. Today, bishops ordain priests so we can go to Confession at our parish.

The gift of Penance, also called Confession or the Sacrament of Reconciliation, is very important to us. Through the Sacrament of Penance, we can regain supernatural life, or grace, in our souls after we have sinned but are sorry for our sins.

Jesus Christ, Son of God, have mercy on me, a sinner!

1. Jesus gave us the Sacrament of _____ to regain God's grace.

2. No matter how serious our sin may be, if we go to God in Confession, truly sorry for our sins, He will always

   _____ us.

3. "Whose sins you shall _____, they are

   _____ them."

When we sin, we offend God very much. There are two kinds of sin: mortal sin and venial sin. Mortal sin is a serious sin against God and completely destroys the life of God's grace within us. When we commit a mortal sin, we knowingly reject God and His Commandments in a serious way. Mortal sin hurts us in a very serious way. We will lose Heaven if we are not sorry for our mortal sin. The way to get God's life in our souls again is to receive the Sacrament of Penance and tell God how sorry we are to have offended Him. If we cannot go to Confession right away, we should tell God how sorry we are by saying a perfect act of contrition.

Venial sins are less serious offenses against the Laws of God. Venial sin does not take away the life of grace from our souls, but venial sin saddens God. Venial sins make us less pleasing to God. When we fight with our brothers and sisters, we hurt God. When we commit a venial sin, we lessen the amount of grace in our souls, but we do not lose it completely. We should tell God we are sorry, we should ask for His help, and we should try harder to be good.

No amount of venial sins can make us lose God completely. They can never equal a mortal sin, but they will lead us farther and farther from God. The farther we stray from God, the more likely we are to reject God and commit a mortal sin.

The Sacrament of Penance is also called Confession or the Sacrament of Reconciliation.

There are five steps to a good confession:

1) We examine our conscience to remember our sins.

2) We are truly sorry for offending God by our sins.

3) We promise God to try not to commit these sins again.

4) We confess our sins.

5) We do the penance the priest gives us.

A good confession will take away any kind of sin. When we tell God that we are sorry for our sins and do our penance, He gives us many graces to do better and become closer to Him. After each good confession, our souls become white and pure, just like on the day of our Baptism.

Hail, Holy Queen, Mother of Mercy.

1. There are two kinds of sin: _____ sin and _____ sin.

2. Mortal sin completely _____ the life of grace in our souls.

3. To restore God's life in our souls after committing a mortal sin, we must go to _____ and tell God how sorry we are.

Let's go over the steps to a good confession:

1) **We examine our conscience to remember our sins:** The first thing we must do before going to confession is to try to remember all the sins we have committed so that we can confess them. We must examine our conscience by reviewing the Ten Commandments. There are many questions we ought to ask ourselves to examine our conscience:

a) Did I disobey my parents?
   Was I mean or disrespectful to them?

b) Did I say my prayers every day?

c) Did I pay attention at Mass?

d) Did I lie to anyone?

e) Did I steal anything?

f) Was I mean to my playmates or anyone else?

g) Did I get angry? Was I unkind in my anger?

h) Am I kind to everyone I see each day?

2) **We are truly sorry for our sins:** After we have remembered our sins, we must be truly sorry for them. If we are truly sorry, God will forgive us. If we have stolen something, we must return it and be sorry for what we did. Most of all, we are sorry for our sins because we have hurt Jesus, Who loves us so much that He died on the Cross for us. Being sorry for our sins because of our love for God is most pleasing to God. God wants us to be sorry because we offended God Who made us and loves us. God also forgives us if we ask pardon because of our fear of Hell.

3) **We promise God that we will seriously try to not commit these sins again:** We must make a firm decision and a serious attempt to not offend God again. God will give us extra help not to commit them again if we tell Him we love Him, and that we want Him to help us not to sin again, and that we will try very hard not to commit those sins again.

4)	**We confess our sins:** After we have examined our conscience, are truly sorry, and have made a decision to God to try our very best to change, we then go to the priest and confess our sins to him. The priest will never tell anyone our sins. The priest has made a special promise to God that he will never tell anyone the sins he has heard in Confession. We must remember that the priest is taking the place of Jesus in the confessional. When we confess our sins to the priest, we are really confessing them to Jesus and when the priest forgives us, it is really Jesus Who is forgiving us.

5)	**We do the penance the priest gives us:** Finally, the priest will give us a penance. Our penance is usually some prayers we must say to help make up for our sins. The priest might tell you to say the Our Father and the Hail Mary. We must remember our penance. When we leave the confessional, we say our penance before we leave the church.

O God, Thou art powerful; make me a saint.

1.	There are _____ steps to a good confession.

2.	We _____ our conscience to remember our sins.

3.	We examine our conscience by reviewing the _____

	_____.

What happens in the confessional? The confessional is the special place where we tell the priest our sins. After you have prepared yourself for the Sacrament of Penance and are truly sorry for all your sins, you enter the confessional and kneel. You will say, "Bless me Father for I have sinned. It has been (how long) since my last confession." Tell how long it has been since your last confession: two weeks, one month, or however long it has been.

"These are my sins." Then tell your sins to the priest, such as not obeying your mom or dad. Tell how many times you committed that sin.

After telling the priest your sins, say, "I am sorry for these sins and for all the sins of my past life which I have committed and any I have forgotten."

The priest will talk to you. Remember, Jesus Himself is speaking to you through the priest. He tells you how you should try to be better or he may ask you some questions. Then he gives you a penance to say. You say your penance in church after you leave the confessional. The priest then tells you to say an Act of Contrition. Do you know this very important prayer? You should say it each night before going to sleep to tell God that you are sorry for the sins of the day.

ST. JOHN NEPOMUCENE

O my God, I am heartily sorry for having offended Thee, and I detest all my sins because of Thy just punishments. But most of all, because they offend Thee, my God, Who art all good and deserving of all my love. I firmly resolve, with the help of Thy grace, to sin no more, and to avoid the near occasions of sin. Amen.

After saying the Act of Contrition in confession, the priest will speak the words of absolution: "I absolve you from your sins in the Name of the Father, and of the Son, and of the Holy Spirit. Amen."

As we hear the words of absolution, we make the Sign of the Cross. When he is finished, we thank the priest by saying, "Thank you, Father." After we leave the confessional, we should kneel in our pew and say the penance the priest has given us. A great joy will come over us! God has forgiven us and given us His grace. Our souls are pure and clean once again. Try your best not to sin again and stay in the state of grace.

O my Jesus, have mercy on poor sinners like me.

1. The _____ is the place where we confess our sins to the priest.

2. In Confession, the priest takes the place of

   _____.

3. We should say an _____ of _____ each night.

Questions for Week Twenty-two

Day 1:

*   What is the Sacrament of Penance?

Penance is the sacrament by which sins committed after Baptism are forgiven.

Day 2:

* 1. What is actual sin?

Actual sin is any sin that we ourselves commit.

* 2. How many kinds of actual sin are there?

There are two kinds of actual sin: mortal sin and venial sin.

Day 3:

1. What are other names for the Sacrament of Penance?

Confession and the Sacrament of Reconciliation are names for the Sacrament of Penance.

* 2. What must you do to receive the Sacrament of Penance worthily?

To receive the Sacrament of Penance worthily, I must:

   1) Examine my conscience.

   2) Be sorry for my sins.

   3) Make up my mind not to sin again.

   4) Tell my sins to the priest.

   5) Do the penance the priest gives me.

3. May a priest ever tell anyone the sins of Confession?

No, the priest is never allowed to reveal the sins of Confession.

Day 4:

1. The priest takes the place of Whom in the Sacrament of Penance?

   The priest takes the place of Jesus Himself in the Sacrament of Penance.

* 2. How do you make your confession?

   I make my confession in this way:

   1) I go into the confessional and kneel.
   2) I make the Sign of the Cross and say: "Bless me, Father, for I have sinned."
   3) I say: "This is my first confession." (Or, "It has been one week, two weeks, or one month since my last confession.")
   4) I confess my sins.
   5) I listen to what the priest tells me.
   6) I say the Act of Contrition loud enough for the priest to hear me.

3. What is absolution?

   Absolution is the words the priest speaks to forgive our sins.

4. What are the words of absolution?

   The words of absolution are: "I absolve you from your sins in the Name of the Father, and of the Son, and of the Holy Spirit. Amen."

The Holy Eucharist

On Holy Thursday, at the Last Supper, Jesus showed the Apostles how He would be with us always, until the end of time. Jesus gave us a most wonderful sacrament. It is the Holy Eucharist. It is Our Lord Jesus Himself Whom we receive.

At the Last Supper, Our Lord took bread, blessed it, and said, "This is My Body." At that very instant, the bread became His Body. Then Jesus took the cup of wine and said, "This is the cup of My Blood." At once, the wine became His most precious Blood. The bread and wine still looked like bread and wine, but they no longer were. They became the Body and Blood of Jesus Christ. What a great miracle! It is the greatest mystery of all! We cannot see Jesus. We cannot hear Him. But He is truly present. We do not understand how it happens, but we know that it is true because Jesus has told us so.

Whenever you are near the Holy Eucharist, say this prayer:

O Sacrament most holy,
O Sacrament divine,
All praise and all thanksgiving
Be every moment Thine!

After Jesus Christ gave His holy Body and Blood to the Apostles at the Last Supper, He said to them, "Do this in memory of Me." He gave the Apostles the power to do what He did. He gave them the power to change bread and wine into His very Body and Blood. What a wonderful miracle! Our holy priests today take the place of Jesus Christ at every Mass. When the priest says, "This is My Body; this is the cup of My Blood," the little white host and the wine in the chalice truly become the Body and Blood of Christ.

At the Last Supper, Jesus changed bread and wine into His

_____ and _____.

Jesus loves us so much that He wants to be with us always. He is always with us in the Most Blessed Sacrament of the Altar, which is the Holy Eucharist. How happy Jesus is when we visit Him in church and kneel before Him in the tabernacle. He is even more happy when we receive Him with love. He is always with us when we receive Him into our hearts at Holy Communion. When we receive Holy Communion, we truly receive Jesus Christ, Body and Blood, Soul and Divinity. He loves us and wants us to receive Him often.

When we receive Jesus Christ in Holy Communion, our souls must be ready to receive Him. Before our First Holy Communion, we first go to the Sacrament of Penance. We are preparing to have a very special Guest come into our hearts. We must prepare our hearts carefully to receive Jesus. Jesus wants us to be ready to receive Him. We must try hard to be good. We must pay attention at Mass, say our prayers, be obedient to our parents, and ask forgiveness for our sins.

My Jesus, I believe that Thou art truly present in the Most Holy Sacrament of the Altar.

1. When we receive Holy Communion, we truly receive

   _____ _____.

2. When we receive Holy Communion, we receive the Body and
   _____, Soul and Divinity of Jesus Christ.

I must prepare my soul for Jesus Christ Who is about to come to me in Holy Communion. Because receiving Jesus in Holy Communion is so special, I must always be sure my soul is ready. In order to receive Jesus worthily in Holy Communion, I must do three things:

1.   **My soul must be free from mortal sin.** If I have committed a mortal sin, I must first go to Confession. Mortal sin *kills* God's life of grace in the soul. If I do not have this life of grace, there is no place for Jesus to enter into my soul. Before I can invite Jesus into my heart, I must make a place for Him.

I can make this place for Jesus by receiving the Sacrament of Confession. In Confession, the priest has the power to take away the stain of mortal sin. This brings the life of God's grace back in to my soul. Then, there is a place for Jesus to enter.

If I have committed a venial sin, my soul is sick. Jesus wants to heal my soul. He wants it to be well again. Receiving Holy Communion heals the soul. It takes away the wounds of venial sin. Venial sin *wounds* the life of grace. So Jesus can still come into my soul. When He comes, He heals me with His Love.

When I go to Confession, I confess my venial sins also. Confession gives me special graces for fighting sins. These graces make it much easier for me to stop repeating them, so that I offend Jesus less and less in my daily life. Venial sins still hurt Jesus. Venial sin hurts me, too, and the life of grace in my soul. Venial sins make my soul weak, and make it easier for me to commit mortal sin. It is very important to try to stop sinning even in little ways. The special graces of Confession are given to us by God to help us stop sinning.

2.   **I must not eat or drink anything for one hour before receiving Jesus in Holy Communion.** (I may drink water or take medicine anytime.) This shows respect for Jesus in the Blessed Sacrament.

3.   **Before receiving Jesus in Holy Communion, I must think of Him.** I should ask Jesus to come to me. I should say the Act of Contrition. Jesus is coming into my heart, and I should tell Him I love Him. I should tell Him I am sorry for all my sins.

Humbly I will receive Thee, My Jesus.

1. To receive Holy Communion worthily, my soul must be free from

   _____ _____.

2. Before receiving Holy Communion, I should not eat or drink for

   _____ _____.

3. To prepare my soul to receive Jesus, I should say the

   _____ of _____.

At last the wonderful time has come! I have received my Lord and my God in Holy Communion! I must remember there are many angels at every Mass kneeling in adoration before Jesus in the Holy Eucharist. What a loving God I have that He should come into my poor heart!

After receiving Jesus, I return to the pew with my hands folded in prayer. I kneel. I welcome Thee, Jesus, into my heart.

After I receive Jesus in Holy Communion, I should do these things:

1)   I thank Jesus for coming to me.
2)   I tell Him how much I love Him.
3)   I ask Him to help me.
4)   I pray for others.

I tell Jesus I adore Him. I thank Him for coming into my heart. I thank Jesus for all the good things He has given me. Jesus has given me kind and generous parents. He has given me a loving family and a good home. Most of all, He has given me the wonderful gift of my Catholic Faith. I talk to Jesus about all of my needs, and the needs of my family and friends. I ask Him to help me be better so that I may grow in His grace. I ask Our Lord Jesus to bless and help my family and friends.

O my Jesus, I love Thee with my whole heart and soul!

1. After receiving Holy Communion, I _____ Jesus for coming to me.

2. I tell Him how much I _____ Him.

3. I ask Him to _____ me.

4. I _____ for others.

Questions for Week Twenty-three

Day 1:

* 1. What is the Sacrament of the Holy Eucharist?

The Holy Eucharist is the sacrament of the Body and Blood of Our Lord Jesus Christ.

* 2. When does Jesus Christ become present in the Holy Eucharist?

Jesus Christ becomes present in the Holy Eucharist during the Sacrifice of the Mass. *Jesus becomes present when the priest says the words, "This is My Body" and "This is My Blood."*

* 3. Do you receive Jesus Christ in the Sacrament of the Holy Eucharist?

I do receive Jesus Christ in the Sacrament of the Holy Eucharist when I receive Holy Communion.

Day 2:

1. May a person receive Holy Communion if he has mortal sin on his soul?

No, a person must not receive Holy Communion if he has mortal sin on his soul.

2. If a person has a mortal sin on his soul, what sacrament must he first receive before going to Holy Communion?

A person in mortal sin must first receive the Sacrament of Penance.

3. Do you see Jesus Christ in the Holy Eucharist?

No, I do not see Jesus Christ in the Holy Eucharist because He is hidden under the appearances of bread and wine.

Day 3:

*   What must you do to receive Holy Communion?

To receive Holy Communion, I must

1) Have my soul free from mortal sin.

2) Not eat or drink anything for one hour before Holy Communion. Water or medicine may be taken at any time before Holy Communion.

Day 4:

* 1. What should I do before Holy Communion?
      Before Holy Communion I should:

     1) Think of Jesus.

     2) Say the prayers I have learned.

     3) Ask Jesus to come to me.

2. How can we unite with Jesus if we cannot go to Communion?
    We can unite with Jesus by making a spiritual communion.

3. What are the sacred places in church?
    The altar is a very sacred place in the church because the Sacrifice of Jesus is renewed there daily for the salvation of the world.

    The tabernacle is a very sacred place in the church because Our Lord, Body, Blood, Soul, and Divinity, is truly present in the tabernacle.

Confirmation, Holy Orders, Matrimony, and Anointing of the Sick

The sacraments are seven outward ways that Jesus Christ gave us to receive Sanctifying Grace into our souls. Do you remember what grace is? Grace is the life of God within us. The only way that we can go to Heaven is to have Jesus Christ's own life in our souls. That is called being in the *state of grace*. Jesus gave us the seven sacraments while He was still on Earth. We have already learned about three of them: Baptism, Penance, and Holy Eucharist. In this chapter, we will learn about the four other sacraments. These are Confirmation, Holy Orders, Holy Matrimony, and Anointing of the Sick.

Confirmation

Usually, we receive Confirmation when we become young adults at about twelve years old. All of the sacraments fill us with the Holy Spirit. In Confirmation, the Holy Spirit comes to us in a special way. We usually receive the Sacrament of Confirmation from the bishop. In Confirmation, the Holy Spirit gives us special gifts that help us to live our Faith more strongly, to defend it, and to teach it to others. The Holy Spirit makes us strong like soldiers, to sacrifice for Jesus if it is needed. Confirmation makes us soldiers in the army of Christ. We join the army of Christ to guard and defend the Catholic Faith with our very lives, if we are ever called to do so.

We must try to spread the Faith to others because only the Catholic Faith has *all* God's truths. Confirmation helps us love our Faith the way the Apostles did on Pentecost Sunday. Do you remember what happened that day? On Pentecost, the Apostles were so filled with the Holy Spirit that they bravely preached God's truths to the people. They were no longer afraid. From the Holy Spirit, they received the courage to tell everyone about Jesus. What great love they had for the Faith! They were on fire for Jesus Christ. The Holy Spirit gave them that love, and in Confirmation, the Holy Spirit will give us that very same burning love for Jesus Christ and His Church.

Blessed be God,
in His angels and in His saints!

1. In the Sacrament of _____, we receive the Holy Spirit in a special way.

2. We usually receive the Sacrament of Confirmation from the

   _____.

3. In Confirmation, we become _____ in the army

   of _____.

Holy Orders

Holy Orders is the sacrament by which men become priests. A priest is a man not like other men. He belongs to God alone. The Sacrament of Holy Orders is very special because only a priest can unite with Jesus to offer the Holy Sacrifice of the Mass. Only a priest is given the power by Jesus to change bread and wine into the Body and Blood of Jesus Christ. Only a priest has the power by Jesus to forgive sins in the Sacrament of Penance. The priest takes the place of Jesus at every Mass. He shares in the priesthood of Jesus Christ. It is a wonderful privilege that God gives only to men.

A boy should listen carefully as he prays so that God can tell him if He wants him for His special work in the priesthood. Becoming an altar boy is a very good way to become close to Jesus. Many priests were once altar boys. God will give the boys He chooses the grace to respond when He calls.

The Sacrament of Holy Orders is reserved for men. Only a man can become a priest. Do you know why? A priest takes the place of Jesus. Since Jesus Christ was a man, only a man can be made a priest.

Our vocation, God's choice of life for us, is something very important. We are all called to be saints in Heaven one day, no matter what we are called to be while we are on Earth. A man may be called to the priesthood, the religious life, the single life, or to become the father of a family. A woman may become a religious sister, a married woman raising children, or have a vocation to the single state. The important thing is to be the best in whatever our state in life might be. Whatever we may become, we should offer our lives to God, making our lives holy and pleasing to Our Lord.

Lord, grant us priests;
Lord, grant us many priests;
Lord, grant us many holy priests.

1. Holy Orders is the sacrament by which _____ become

   _____.

2. Only a _____ can receive Holy Orders.

3. Each one of us is called to be a _____.

Matrimony

Like Holy Orders, the Sacrament of Matrimony is another calling that God gives. In this vocation, God gives a man and a woman the graces they need to make a good and loving home and family. The man should imitate St. Joseph and the woman should try to be like Mary, Our Blessed Mother. If they try to live like the Holy Family, God will bless them with peace and happiness. Children are the special gift that God sends to many marriages. He sends children so that the parents will teach them how to know, love, and serve God.

This is the calling that God gave to your parents. In the Sacrament of Matrimony, your parents stood in front of the priest and promised each other to live together in God's love and raise a family. They promised to be married for life, until one of them dies; their marriage will last as long as both of them are living. God gave them many special graces on their wedding day. He gave them the grace to help each other love God and to help each other get to Heaven.

The greatest gift that God gave to your parents is you! What joy your parents have in teaching you how to love God! Thank your parents every day for showing you how to love Jesus. Try very hard to be good and to imitate the Child Jesus in obeying your parents, so that your whole family may live the way the Holy Family lived. In this way, you can be happy with Jesus in Heaven forever!

Jesus, Mary, and Joseph, pray for my family.

1. In the Sacrament of _____, a man and woman join together for life.

2. To make a loving family, each member should try to imitate the

   _____ _____.

3. God sends children so parents will teach them how to _____,

   _____, and _____ God.

Anointing of the Sick

Do you remember the name of the sacrament you received as a baby that made you a member of God's Church? It was the Sacrament of Baptism. At that time, you were given the life of God's grace in your soul. The Sacrament of Baptism prepares us for the beginning of our lives as Catholics. God has given us another sacrament that prepares us with grace when we are gravely ill or at the end of our lives. It helps us to be ready for Heaven. This sacrament is called Anointing of the Sick. It is also known as Extreme Unction.

When a person is very sick or injured, or very old, or if a doctor says a person is near death, the priest comes to him and anoints him with holy oil. The priest then gives the dying person a special Confession to forgive any last sins that he has before he dies. If the sick person is truly sorry for all the sins of his whole life, then his soul becomes clean and pure. If the dying person is able to receive Holy Communion, then the priest gives him Our Lord in the Holy Eucharist one last time. This Eucharist is given in the last moments of a dying person's life as a special help in leaving this life and entering the next. What a peaceful way to meet Jesus in the life that comes after death!

The Sacrament of Anointing of the Sick brings many extra graces to a seriously ill or dying person. This sacrament gives us the strength to endure the suffering that comes before death. This sacrament takes away venial sins. It can take away mortal sins if the suffering person is too ill to go to Confession, but is sorry for his sins. Anointing of the Sick gives a special grace which frees us from the need to do penance for our sins in Purgatory. It comforts us when we are gravely ill or in our last hours. Anointing of the Sick makes a person brave to face God after death and worship Him with his whole heart.

Sometimes Anointing of the Sick will restore health and strength to the body. Anointing of the Sick may be received whenever it is necessary, and more than once if a person recovers and then become very sick again. For those who are ready to leave this world and join the angels and saints in Heaven, the Anointing prepares them for this meeting. How wonderful for God to give us such an important sacrament right before we die. How happy we will be to meet God with a pure and clean soul!

Heart of Jesus, have mercy on the dying.

1. The Sacrament of _____ _____ _____

   _____ helps a person before dying.

2. The Sacrament of Anointing of the Sick gives a person

   _____ to endure any suffering that may come before death.

3. Sometimes, Anointing of the Sick can restore _____ to a dying person.

Questions for Week Twenty-four

Day 1:

* 1. What does grace do to the soul?

  Grace makes the soul holy and pleasing to God.

  2. How many sacraments are there?

  There are seven sacraments.

* 3. What will Confirmation do for you?

  Confirmation, through the coming of the Holy Spirit, will make me a soldier of Jesus Christ.

Day 2:

  1. What is the sacrament by which men become priests and bishops?

  Holy Orders is the sacrament by which men become priests.

  2. What are the chief powers of a priest given by Jesus Christ?

  The chief powers of a priest given by Jesus Christ are to forgive sins and to change bread and wine into the Body and Blood of Jesus Christ.

Day 3:

1. What is a vocation?

   A vocation is a calling from God to each person to choose a certain way of life.

2. What is the vocation God gave my parents?

   God called my parents to the vocation of the married life.

* 3. What is the Sacrament of Matrimony?

   Matrimony is the sacrament by which a baptized man and a baptized woman bind themselves for life in a lawful marriage and receive the grace to discharge their duties.

Day 4:

1. Which sacrament prepares us for death?

   The Sacrament of Anointing of the Sick prepares us for death.

2. What is the main purpose of the sacrament?

   The main purpose of the sacrament is to prepare a dying person to meet God, by giving him many special graces.

The Holy Sacrifice of the Mass

Jesus is with us in the Holy Eucharist offered at every Mass. The Holy Sacrifice of the Mass is the most important event that happens each day. We should try to attend daily Mass, if we are able, and receive Our Lord Jesus in Holy Communion.

We know that the most important part of the Mass is called the Consecration. With the words, "This is My Body" and "This is the cup of My Blood," the priest changes the bread and wine into the Body and Blood of Jesus. The whole Mass leads to this most holy and glorious miracle. The Church has told us that angels are present at every Mass. They surround the altar and fill the church. They sing heavenly hymns of praise to God. We cannot see or hear these beautiful angels because they are pure spirits, but they are present just the same. What a glorious moment! We must treat Jesus in the Holy Eucharist with the same reverence and glory as do the beautiful angels and saints in Heaven.

Let us learn about each part of the Mass so that we can properly prepare ourselves for the coming of Jesus Christ in the miracle of the Holy Eucharist.

Blessed be Jesus in the Most Holy Sacrament of the altar!

1. The Holy Sacrifice of the _____ is the most important event that happens each day.

2. The most important part of the Mass is the _____.

3. We cannot see the angels present at every Mass because they are

   pure _____.

The Mass is a Sacrifice. It is the re-presentation of the Sacrifice Jesus made when He died on the Cross. The same Sacrifice of Jesus is made present at Mass on the altar.

It is Jesus Christ offering Himself as a Sacrifice to God His Father to make up for the sins of everyone in the world. Jesus makes this Sacrifice in all the Masses in the world out of love for God His Father, and out of love for all of us. It is the unbloody Sacrifice. Our Lord sacrificed Himself to His Heavenly Father by suffering and dying on the Cross for our sins on Good Friday, about two thousand years ago.

In the Mass, Our Lord offers Himself to His Father once more, but in an unbloody manner. When we say "unbloody Sacrifice," we mean that Jesus does not die as He did on Calvary, once and for all. Rather, His Sacrifice is made present in an "unbloody" way. The Holy Eucharist is truly His Body and Blood. That is what Jesus said at the Last Supper. Jesus is the chief Priest in the Mass, but He uses the words, the actions, the mind, and the will of the priest we see at the altar. Although we do not see Jesus, He is truly present. Jesus offers Himself to God the Father through the priest we see at Mass.

Jesus told His Apostles to continue this wonderful miracle. This is the Mass.

Lamb of God, Who takes away the sins of the world, have mercy on us.

1. The Mass is a _____.

2. In the Mass, Jesus offers Himself in an _____ manner.

3. Jesus offers Himself to God through the _____ at Mass.

The Mass is the same Sacrifice as the Sacrifice of the Cross. We should be as reverent at Mass as if we were seeing Jesus die for our sins on the Cross at Calvary about two thousand years ago.

On the Cross, Jesus died in pain and suffering. His Sacrifice on the first Good Friday was a bloody one. After His death, Our Lord rose from the dead. He will never suffer and die again. In the Mass, Our Lord does not suffer and die. Our Lord's Sacrifice in the Mass is an unbloody Sacrifice. Still, the two Sacrifices are the same. The Sacrifice of the Mass and the Sacrifice of the Cross are the same because the Victim, Jesus Christ, is the same. This is what Jesus Himself has taught us.

Most Holy Trinity, Father, Son, and Holy Spirit, I adore You profoundly and offer You the Most Precious Body, Blood, Soul, and Divinity of Jesus Christ, present in all the tabernacles of the world, in reparation for all the outrages, sacrileges, and indifference by which He Himself is offended. And by the infinite merits of His Most Sacred Heart and of the Immaculate Heart of Mary, I beg of you the conversion of poor sinners.*

1. The Mass is the same Sacrifice as the Sacrifice of the

    _____.

2. Our Lord's Sacrifice at Calvary was a _____ one.

3. Our Lord's Sacrifice at Mass is an _____ one.

*Prayer taught by the angel to the three children of Fatima.

At the Consecration of the Mass, the priest offers Jesus to God the Father. Then a wonderful thing happens: just as Jesus gave Himself to His Apostles at the Last Supper, so in the Mass, the priest gives us Jesus in Holy Communion.

"Give us this day our daily bread."

When we receive Our Lord Jesus in Holy Communion, we truly receive His Body and Blood, Soul and Divinity.

We must receive Holy Communion with perfect reverence. Let us remember Who it is that we are really receiving. When we return to our pews, we kneel to thank God for coming to us. The priest says prayers of thanks. The priest then gives us the final blessing.

When Mass is over, we should not be in a hurry to leave. We have just received Our Lord Jesus, the Son of God. We have become a living tabernacle for Our Lord. We should stay a few minutes longer in our pew and visit with Jesus. We should bring Him all our joys and cares. He wants us to come to Him with all our needs and those of our family and friends. We should thank Him for all the good things we have received, especially our Catholic Faith.

When we are ready to leave, we want to use the graces we have just received. We want to love as Jesus did. We want to be kind to everyone we meet. We shall not complain. We shall live our Faith every day in every way. The graces of the Mass and Holy Communion will help us to love as Jesus did.

Lord Jesus, shelter our Holy Father, the pope, under the protection of Thy Sacred Heart; be Thou his light, his strength, and his consolation.

The priest gives us _____ in Holy Communion.

Questions for Week Twenty-five

Day 1:

What is the most important part of the Mass?

The Consecration is the most important part of the Mass.

Day 2:

What is the Mass?

The Mass is the re-presentation of the Sacrifice of Jesus suffering and dying on the Cross. Jesus is truly present on the altar.

Day 3:

1. What happens during the Consecration?

   During the Consecration the priest changes bread and wine into Our Lord's Body and Blood. This takes place when he says, "This is My Body" and "This is the cup of My Blood."

2. How is the Mass like Calvary?

   In the Mass, Our Lord renews His Sacrifice on Calvary of Himself to God the Father for our sins. The Sacrifice of the Mass is an unbloody Sacrifice.

The Church That Christ Founded

Do you remember the story of our first parents, Adam and Eve? When they sinned, they could no longer be with God in the beautiful Garden of Paradise. They lost God's grace because of their sin, and the gates of Heaven were closed. No one could enter Heaven after the sin of Adam and Eve.

When Our Lord Jesus died on the Cross, He made up to God for the sins of mankind. God the Father was pleased with His Son's perfect Sacrifice. Our Lord Jesus opened the gates of Heaven to us once again. Then Jesus returned to His Father in Heaven to prepare a place for us there. How loving is Our Lord Jesus! However, it is still not easy for us to enter Heaven. We would not know how to enter Heaven on our own. Only Jesus could show us. Jesus did not leave us alone here on Earth, not knowing the way to Heaven. He loves us too much for that. Before Jesus left the Earth, He started the Catholic Church so that all men could obtain Sanctifying Grace. Everyone needs Sanctifying Grace in order to enter Heaven.

Do you know how we receive Sanctifying Grace through the Catholic Church? We receive Sanctifying Grace through the seven sacraments. Only the Catholic Church has the seven sacraments, which are the sure means to Heaven.

O God, come to my assistance!

1. Our Lord's death on the Cross atoned to God for the

   _____ of mankind.

2. Our Lord's death on the Cross was a perfect _____.

3. It is still not _____ for us to get to Heaven.

Someday our bodies must die. However, our souls never die. Our souls will live forever. If we love God and stay in His grace, we will be rewarded by being happy in Heaven with God forever. We are able to enter Heaven only if we are free from all sin. We can rid our souls of sin by the graces we can obtain through the sacraments.

Those people in Heaven are free from any trace of sin. They are filled with God's grace. They pray for us on Earth so that someday we can join them in happiness with God. Many of those in Heaven did not go to Heaven right after they died. Their souls were not pure enough to enter into the presence of the Blessed Trinity. They first had to go to a place to be purified. That place is called Purgatory.

If you die with Sanctifying Grace in your soul, your soul will go either to Heaven or Purgatory. Heaven is for those who no longer have sin on their soul. If you have venial sins on your soul at death, your soul is not perfect. Purgatory is the place where souls go who are not ready to enter the gates of Heaven. Souls must go to Purgatory until they make up for their sins.

All of the souls in Purgatory belong to Our Lord's Church. That is why they are known as the holy souls. Even though they suffer, they are filled with joy because they know they will someday enter Heaven. We need to pray for the holy souls. Our prayers can make their time in Purgatory shorter.

We pray to Our Blessed Mother and the saints in Heaven so that they will help us to love God as they do. We ask them to help us reject sin. We read the lives of the saints to see how they stayed away from sin. How wonderful it is for us to imitate their lives!

The Catholic Church includes three groups of people: the saints in Heaven, called the Church Triumphant; the souls in Purgatory, called the Church Suffering; and all of its members on Earth, called the Church Militant. We are all part of the Catholic Church, which was started by Jesus Christ.

Eternal rest grant unto them, O Lord, and let perpetual light shine upon them.

1. _____ is the place where souls go to be purified before entering Heaven.

2. The Catholic Church includes all the saints in _____, all of the souls in _____, and all of its members on _____.

The Catholic Church has the seven sacraments Jesus gave us. The Catholic Church was started by Jesus Christ. The Catholic Church is made up of people who have been baptized in the Catholic Church. Do you remember that Baptism makes us adopted children of God? All of us who are baptized are united to form God's special family. We are members of His Church, and Jesus is the Head. Jesus sends His grace to us as members of His Church. Each of us has a special place in God's family, the Catholic Church.

All Catholics are joined in four ways:

1) **We have the same true Faith.** We believe all that Jesus taught.

2) **We have the same Sacrifice.** It is the Holy Sacrifice of the Mass.

3) **We have the same sacraments.** Jesus gave us seven sacraments.

4) **We are united under one and the same visible head on Earth,** our Holy Father, the pope. The pope is the head of Christ's Church on Earth.

Jesus is the invisible Head of all of us here on Earth. Jesus is the Head of the members of the Church in Purgatory. Jesus is the Head of all the saints in Heaven.

Jesus is the Head of the Church. Jesus knew we would also need a head of the Church on Earth after He returned to Heaven. He knew we would need someone who knows all the things that Jesus taught and can teach them to us. We need someone on Earth to show us how to get to Heaven. That is why Jesus gave His Church on Earth a head. We call this head the pope, or the Holy Father.

Before He returned to Heaven, Jesus chose St. Peter to be the head of His Church on Earth. St. Peter was the first pope. He was a loving Holy Father to the first Christians, teaching them all about Jesus and ruling the Church. Jesus continues to choose a pope, a leader for His Church. The Catholic Church still has a Holy Father, the pope, who teaches us about Jesus and carefully guides us on the road to Heaven.

Jesus, Mary, and Joseph, I love You. Save souls.

1. The _____ _____ is the Church founded by Jesus Christ.

2. St. Peter was the first _____.

Our Lord Jesus gave us a wonderful promise about His Church. He said that "the gates of Hell shall not prevail against it." This means that the Catholic Church can never be destroyed. The Catholic Church is the Church that Jesus established, or started. The Catholic Church is the one true Church of Jesus Christ. When the Catholic Church teaches us in matters of Faith, such as the sacraments, the Creed, or the Ten Commandments, it can never teach anything wrong.

Whenever the Holy Father, the pope, speaks as the head of the entire Church, and gives an official teaching on matters of faith or morals, he cannot make a mistake. The Holy Spirit protects the Holy Father in a special way. Jesus, the invisible Head of the Church, guides the pope, the visible head of the Church on Earth.

Our Lady of Fatima, guide and protect our Holy Father.

1. The gates of Hell shall not _____ against the Catholic Church.

2. The Catholic Church is the one _____ Church started by Jesus Christ.

3. The visible head of the Catholic Church is the _____.

4. The invisible Head of the Catholic Church is _____.

Questions for Week Twenty-six

Day 1:

1. Why were the gates of Heaven closed to all?

   The gates of Heaven were closed to all because of Adam and Eve's sin.

2. Where did the souls of the Just go before the gates of Heaven were opened?

   The souls of the Just waited for the gates of Heaven to be opened in a place of natural happiness without seeing God.

3. Who opened the gates of Heaven once again?

   Jesus Christ opened the gates of Heaven once again by His sufferings and death on the Cross.

Day 2:

1. Can I enter Heaven if there is any trace of sin on my soul?

   No, I cannot enter Heaven if there is any trace of sin on my soul.

2. Where do souls go to be purified if they die with venial sin?

   Souls go to Purgatory if they die with venial sin.

3. How can we help the holy souls in Purgatory?

   We can help the holy souls in Purgatory by offering our prayers, sufferings, and acts of self-denial to lessen their time of suffering. We can help them greatly by having Masses offered for them. We should pray for the dead members of our family.

Day 3:

How can we avoid Purgatory?

We can avoid Purgatory by prayers, by acts of self-denial, and by attending Holy Mass.

Day 4:

Who are the members of the Catholic Church that Christ founded?

The members of the Catholic Church that Christ founded are three:

1) The Church Militant (those still alive on Earth),

2) The Church Suffering (the souls in Purgatory),

3) And the Church Triumphant (the saints in Heaven).

Fourth Quarter

Our Blessed Mother and the Rosary

We are all very blessed, because Jesus gave us His very own Mother.

Jesus gave Our Blessed Mother Mary to us at the foot of the Cross. She was a great comfort to Jesus as He was dying. While He was being nailed to the Cross, His Mother Mary remained at His side. St. John the Apostle was there too. One of the last things Jesus said was to St. John. Jesus looked down at John from the Cross and said, "Behold thy mother." That is, "She is *your* mother now." Jesus gave His Mother Mary to John and to all of us too. Our Blessed Mother is ready to help us whenever we need her. She loves us and watches over us. She wants to help us enter Heaven.

A long time ago, there lived a holy priest named Dominic. He loved Jesus and Our Lady very much. He tried very hard to make others love them. He wanted people to repent for their sins. Dominic prayed to the Virgin Mary for help, and she answered him. In the classic book *Lives of the Saints* by Father Alan Butler, in 1208, Father wrote that the Blessed appeared to St. Dominic in the little chapel of Notre Dame. She was holding a rosary in her hand, then gave it to him. It is believed that she said, "Offer this prayer for sinners. It is a powerful weapon." St. Dominic started saying the Rosary and began teaching others to say it as well. More and more people returned to God through the power of the prayers of the Rosary. Our Lady wants us to say the Rosary every day, as she told the three children when she appeared to them at Fatima.

Queen of the Most Holy Rosary, pray for us.

1. Jesus gave each of us His _____ as He was dying on the Cross.

2. Our Lady gave the Rosary to _____ _____.

The Joyful Mysteries

The Five Joyful Mysteries of the Rosary celebrate the happy events of Mary and Jesus before Jesus suffered on the Cross.

First Joyful Mystery: The Annunciation of the Archangel Gabriel to Mary

The Archangel Gabriel was sent by God the Father to ask Mary to be the Mother of His Son, Jesus Christ. Mary humbly accepted by saying, "I am the handmaid of the Lord." A handmaid is like a servant girl who does the will of her master. Mary would do whatever God wished.

Second Joyful Mystery: The Visitation

The Archangel Gabriel told Mary that her cousin Elizabeth was going to have a baby. Mary wanted to help her cousin, so she traveled to her cousin's home in another town. St. Elizabeth, who lived a holy life, already knew that Mary was to be the Mother of the Savior. When Mary arrived, Elizabeth said, "Blessed art thou among women, and blessed is the fruit of thy womb." She also said, "Who am I that the mother of my Lord should come to me?"

Third Joyful Mystery: The Nativity, or Birth of Our Lord

Though Jesus is God and the Son of God the Father, He chose to be born in a poor stable in Bethlehem. On that first Christmas day, the shepherds in the nearby fields came to worship Him. They worshiped Him because angels told them Jesus was the Savior mankind had been waiting for since the time of Adam and Eve.

Fourth Joyful Mystery: The Presentation of the Child Jesus in the Temple

It was the Jewish law that parents present, or dedicate, their first son to God shortly after birth. Mary and Joseph met the holy man Simeon at the Temple. He took Baby Jesus in his arms, and praised God because he recognized that Jesus was the promised Savior.

Fifth Joyful Mystery: The Finding of the Child Jesus in the Temple

When Jesus was twelve years old, the Holy Family went to Jerusalem for a holy feast. Afterwards, when traveling back, Mary and Joseph discovered that Jesus was not with any of the travelers. They could not find Jesus for three days. Finally, they found Him back in the Temple in Jerusalem, teaching the priests and teachers. He obediently returned home with His parents.

Blessed be the name of Mary, Virgin and Mother.

1. The Archangel _____ was sent by God to Mary.

2. Elizabeth knew that Mary was to be the Mother of the

_____.

3. Mary and Joseph found Jesus _____ in the Temple.

The Luminous Mysteries

In 2002, Pope John Paul II wrote a letter to all Catholics. This was a special letter about the Rosary. The Holy Father asked everyone to pray the Rosary each day. He wrote that parents and children should pray the Rosary together as a family.

Pope John Paul II wanted us to think carefully about the most important times during the three years of Our Lord's public life. So, the pope added another set of mysteries to the Rosary. The new mysteries are called Luminous, which means full of light, because they are about very special times in the life of Jesus, the Light of the world. These events can "shed light" or give us more understanding about Jesus. The pope wrote that he thought that the greatest events of Our Lord's public life should have a place in the Rosary. The Luminous Mysteries are said on Thursdays between the Glorious and Sorrowful Mysteries.

First Luminous Mystery: The Baptism of Our Lord

Our Lord went to the River Jordan, where John the Baptist was baptizing the people and telling them to do penance. He was preparing them for the coming of Our Lord. When John saw Jesus, he cried out: "Behold the Lamb of God! Behold Him Who takes away the sins of the world!" Though Jesus did not need Baptism because He is God and sinless, He told John to baptize Him to show that we all need Baptism. The sky opened and the Holy Spirit, in the form of a dove, rested on Him. God the Father spoke from the clouds, saying, "This is My beloved Son, in Whom I am well pleased." This was the beginning of Our Lord's public life.

Second Luminous Mystery: The Wedding at Cana

Jesus and His Mother were invited to a wedding at Cana. When the wine at the feast ran out, Our Lady wanted to help the bride and groom. She went to Jesus. She knew He could fix the problem because He is God. She told the waiters, "Do whatever He tells you." Jesus had them fill the wine jugs with water. When the steward tasted it, he said to the groom, "You have saved the best wine for now." Jesus changed the water into wine! He worked His first public miracle at His Mother's request.

Third Luminous Mystery: Jesus Proclaims the Coming of the Kingdom of God

When Jesus began His mission to preach the Gospel to people, He went into the synagogue and read from Isaias the Prophet. He found the place where it was written, "The Spirit of the Lord is upon Me. He has anointed me to preach the Gospel to the poor, to heal the sorrowful of heart, and to heal the blind." With this, Jesus revealed the Kingdom of God to the people, and made it known that He was the one about whom Isaias had written. He told the people to be sorry for their sins and to believe in Him.

Fourth Luminous Mystery: The Transfiguration

Jesus went to the top of Mount Tabor to pray with Peter, James, and John. While He was praying, His face began to change and His clothing became glittering and pure white. Moses and Elias, appeared in majesty with Jesus. As the Apostles looked on, a cloud came and covered them all. A voice spoke out of the cloud saying, "This is My beloved Son. Listen to Him." Jesus revealed Himself in all His heavenly glory to His three closest Apostles.

Fifth Luminous Mystery: The Institution of the Holy Eucharist (The Last Supper)

The night before Our Savior died, He brought the Apostles together at the Last Supper. In the Upper Room, He changed bread and wine into His Body and Blood. Out of His great love for us, He gave us the Sacrament of the Holy Eucharist. At the Last Supper, Jesus made the Apostles priests so that they could bring us Jesus, even after He ascended into Heaven. Our Lord will be with us, in the Eucharist, until the end of the world.

Blessed are the pure of heart, for they shall see God.

The Sorrowful Mysteries

The Five Sorrowful Mysteries remind us of the Passion and death of Jesus Christ.

First Sorrowful Mystery: The Agony of Our Lord in the Garden

After the Last Supper, Jesus went to the Garden of Gethsemane to pray. He prayed to His Father in Heaven. He wept for the sins of everyone, from Adam and Eve to the last person on Earth. He suffered so much for poor sinners who offend God that He sweat blood.

Second Sorrowful Mystery: The Scourging at the Pillar

The bad soldiers had arrested Jesus and taken Him to prison. In the prison, they scourged Him. This means they beat Him with whips. Jesus suffered this to make up to God the Father for all the sins of all people, past, present, and future.

Third Sorrowful Mystery: The Crowning with Thorns

Jesus was called King of the Jews by the people. The soldiers made fun of Jesus by forcing a crown of thorns on His sacred Head.

Fourth Sorrowful Mystery: The Carrying of the Cross

Jesus carried the Cross through the streets of Jerusalem and up the hill to Calvary. Jesus fell three times along the way. Simon helped Him carry His Cross. He met His Mother Mary. He met Veronica who wiped His face with her veil.

Fifth Sorrowful Mystery: The Crucifixion and Death of Our Lord

Jesus was nailed by His hands and His feet to the Cross. He hung on the Cross for three hours before He died. He asked God the Father to forgive those who crucified Him because "they know not what they do."

Christ above in torment hangs, She beneath beholds the pangs Of her dying glorious Son.

1. In the Garden of Gethsemane, Jesus _____ blood.

2. Jesus suffered the scourging for the sins of all _____.

3. Jesus asked God the Father to _____ those who crucified Him.

The Glorious Mysteries

The Five Glorious Mysteries recall the glorious events in the lives of Our Lord Jesus and His Mother Mary after His death on the Cross.

First Glorious Mystery: The Resurrection of Our Lord

On the first Easter morning, Jesus rose from the dead. Jesus appeared to Mary Magdalen when she was at the tomb. He appeared to His Apostles in the Upper Room. He appeared to two of His disciples on the road to Emmaeus, and explained to them about the Resurrection. Jesus rose from the tomb in glory to prove that He is truly God. His Resurrection shows us that we too will rise from the dead at the end of the world.

Second Glorious Mystery: The Ascension of Jesus into Heaven

After spending forty days on Earth teaching His Apostles and disciples, Jesus took them to the top of a mountain. Many people followed Jesus. There, they watched Him leave the ground and rise up high into the clouds until they could no longer see Him. As they stood there watching the sky, an angel appeared and assured them that one day, Jesus would return to Earth. When Jesus returns at the end of the world, He will come in glory.

Third Glorious Mystery:
The Descent of the Holy Spirit upon the Apostles and Our Lady

Jesus had promised that after He returned to Heaven, He would send the Third Person of the Blessed Trinity, the Holy Spirit. On Pentecost Sunday, as the Apostles and the Blessed Mother prayed in the Upper Room, the Holy Spirit came down upon their heads as tongues of fire. The Holy Spirit filled them with courage, wisdom, and many miraculous powers.

Fourth Glorious Mystery:
The Assumption of the Blessed Virgin Mary into Heaven

The Blessed Mother helped the Apostles for many years. Finally, it was time for her to go to Heaven. Because she had no sin on her soul, God would not let His Blessed Mother's pure body remain on Earth. God raised her body and soul to Heaven. There, Mary and Jesus wait for us. As our loving heavenly Mother, she will go to Jesus for us with all our cares.

Fifth Glorious Mystery:
Coronation of the Blessed Mother as Queen of Heaven and Earth

When the Blessed Mother arrived in Heaven, all the angels and saints welcomed her as their Queen. The Blessed Trinity lovingly crowned her as Queen over all creation. Because of her holiness and obedience, she sits beside her Divine Son, Jesus Christ, the King of Heaven and Earth.

Hail! Holy Queen enthroned above!
Hail! Mother of mercy and of love!

Holy Days of Obligation

Do you remember which of the Ten Commandments tells us that we must go to Mass on Sundays? The Third Commandment says, "Remember, keep holy the Lord's Day." This means we must go to Mass on Sundays and on holy days of obligation. In the United States, there are six holy days of obligation during the year. The Church obliges us to go to Mass on each one of them. God wants us to celebrate holy days as if they were Sundays by going to the Holy Sacrifice of the Mass and by keeping the feast day holy. We should avoid all unnecessary servile work, and avoid all unnecessary shopping on holy days of obligation. Can you name the six holy days? They are:

January 1	Mary, the Mother of God
40 days after Easter	The Ascension of Our Lord into Heaven
August 15	The Assumption of Our Lady into Heaven
November 1	All Saints' Day
December 8	The Immaculate Conception
December 25	Christmas Day

This week, we will learn about these six feast days and why they are important.

January 1: Mary, Mother of God

The first holy day of the year comes on the first day of the year, New Year's Day. On this day, we honor Mary as the Mother of God. She brought our dear Jesus into the world. Jesus is God, and Mary is the Mother of Jesus; therefore, Mary is the Mother of God. She deserves so much devotion. She is the Mother of God and the Mother of us all. She loves each and every one of us. On January 1, we honor her by going to Mass and showing reverence to her under her most holy title, the Mother of God.

Holy Mary, Mother of God, pray for us sinners.

1. There are _____ holy days of obligation in the United States.

2. We should celebrate holy days of obligation as if they were

   _____.

3. We honor Our Lady's feast day as Mary, Mother of God, on

   _____ _____.

Forty Days after Easter: Ascension Thursday

The Ascension of Our Lord is always celebrated forty days after Easter, and it is always on a Thursday. After Christ rose from the dead, He stayed on Earth for forty days before He ascended into Heaven.

August 15: The Assumption

The Assumption of Our Lady into Heaven is celebrated on August 15. Although the words Ascension and Assumption are similar, they do not mean the same thing. Jesus ascended into Heaven by His own power because He is God. He took Himself up to Heaven. Mary could not take herself up to Heaven because she is only human. Jesus took her to Heaven. She was assumed, that is, taken up into Heaven by God.

The Ascension and the Assumption are two of the greatest feast days of the Church. There are many beautiful customs which people follow to honor these great holy days. On Ascension Thursday, be sure to honor Our Lord's triumphant return to His heavenly throne forty days after Easter. Remember to show Mary how much you love her on August 15, the Feast of the Assumption by keeping her feast day special.

Remember that you must attend Mass on each holy day of obligation.

Where Our Lady is honored as Queen, Our Lord will be revered as King.

1. On _____ Thursday we honor Our Lord's return to Heaven.

2. On the Feast of the _____, we honor Our Lady's body and soul being carried to Heaven.

3. On the holy days of obligation, we must attend _____.

November 1: All Saints' Day

November 1 is the Feast of All Saints. There are many known saints in Heaven. There are many unknown saints in Heaven. All who go to Heaven are saints. Some reach Heaven after a period of suffering in Purgatory. Some spent their lives in total love of God and went straight to Heaven after death. The great saints we know loved God more than they loved themselves. Many of them shed their blood and gave their lives for God as martyrs. Now they are all God's friends in Heaven.

There are many saints in Heaven whom we do not know. Our relatives and friends who have died in the state of grace have the promise of Heaven. If they have reached Heaven, they are numbered among the saints. On the Feast of All Saints' Day, the Catholic Church honors everyone who has gained Heaven, all the well-known saints as well as those known only to God.

All Saints' Day is a good day to make up our minds to be saints. Each of us has a patron saint. We should pray to our patron saint every day. We should learn about the holy life our patron saint has led and try to be just as holy. What joy there is in Heaven on All Saints' Day! How happy the saints are to be with God and how much they want for us to be good in order that we may join them in Heaven someday!

All ye angels, saints, apostles, and martyrs, pray for us!

1. The Feast of All Saints is on _____ _____.

2. Everyone who is in Heaven is considered a

   _____.

3. On All Saints' Day, we honor the _____ in Heaven.

165

December 8: The Immaculate Conception

Do you know whom we call the Immaculate Conception? The Blessed Virgin Mary is the Immaculate Conception because she was conceived without Original Sin. When Mary was conceived in the womb of her mother, St. Anne, He kept Original Sin away from her pure soul. Mary is so pure and good that she never committed a sin. On December 8, Our Lord wants us to honor His dear Mother in a special way. On this day, we go to Mass to celebrate our heavenly Mother's goodness and faithfulness to God. We should spend this feast day honoring Our Lady by special prayers and celebrations.

God is so good for giving His Mother Mary to us. Let us thank God for giving us the Blessed Virgin Mary, who is the Immaculate Conception.

December 25: Christmas

Christ was born on Christmas Day, over two thousand years ago. December 25 is a holy day of obligation. When you awake, before opening your gifts on Christmas Day, kneel before the manger in your home and wish Baby Jesus a happy birthday. When you go to Mass on Christmas morning, approach the image of Baby Jesus in the manger in your church's Nativity scene. Thank Him with all your heart for coming into the world to save us.

O dearest Mother Mary,
prepare my heart for the coming of thy Divine Infant Son.

1. Our Lady is called the _____ _____ because she was conceived without Original Sin.

2. We honor Our Lady's Immaculate Conception on

_____ ____.

3. The Church celebrates the Birth of Our Divine Savior on

_____.

Questions for Week Twenty-nine

Day 1

1. How many holy days of obligation are there?

    There are six holy days of obligation.

2. What are the holy days of obligation in the United States?

    These are the holy days of obligation in the United States:

1)	January 1	Mary, the Mother of God
2)	40 days after Easter	The Ascension of Our Lord
3)	August 15	The Assumption of Our Lady
4)	November 1	All Saints' Day
5)	December 8	The Immaculate Conception
6)	December 25	Christmas Day

Day 2

1. When do we celebrate the Resurrection of Our Lord?

    We celebrate Our Lord's Resurrection on Easter Sunday.

2. What do we call Our Lord's return to Heaven?

    Our Lord's return to Heaven is called the Ascension.

3. What do we call Our Lady's entrance into Heaven?

    Our Lady's entrance into Heaven is called the Assumption.

Day 3

Whom do we honor on November 1?

We honor all the saints in Heaven, those known and unknown, on November 1, All Saints' Day.

Day 4

Why do we call Mary the Immaculate Conception?

We call Mary the Immaculate Conception because she was conceived without Original Sin.

Prayer

The Four Purposes of Prayer

Prayer is the lifting up of our minds and hearts to God. This means that prayer is talking to God. Praying is thinking about God. You can pray anywhere and anytime. God always listens. God is always with you.

There are four reasons to pray. We pray to adore God. We pray to thank God. We pray to tell God we are sorry for our sins. We pray to ask God for special favors.

The chief reason we pray is to adore God. When we make the Sign of the Cross, "In the Name of the Father, and of the Son, and of the Holy Spirit. Amen," we are adoring God, the Blessed Trinity. When we say "Amen," it means that we really believe what we have prayed. Just saying the Name "Jesus" is a powerful prayer.

Whenever we think about God during the day or night, we should say short, silent prayers. Jesus loves to hear them. We say little prayers like, "My Jesus, have mercy," or "Mother of God, pray for us." Each time we pass a Catholic church, we make the Sign of the Cross to show Jesus, "I know You are truly present in the tabernacle inside this church, and I honor You there." Each time we hear the siren of an ambulance or a fire engine, we offer a prayer for the persons the rescue workers are rushing to help. God wants us to pray all the time. In this way, we stay close to God all the time. In this way, we can overcome temptation to sin.

O Jesus, King and Center of all hearts, grant that peace may be in Thy Kingdom.

1. Prayer is the lifting up of our _____ and

   _____ to God.

2. There are _____ reasons to pray.

3. The chief reason we pray is to _____ God.

St. Paul tells us we are to "pray always." God wants us to pray all the time. When we wake in the morning, God's wonderful world greets us. We kneel to say our morning prayers. When we give our whole day to God, our whole day is a prayer right from the start. If we say the Morning Offering, we are offering our whole day up to God as a prayer.

O my Jesus, through the Immaculate Heart of Mary, I offer You all my prayers, works, joys, and sufferings of this day. I offer them for all the intentions of Your Sacred Heart, for the salvation of souls, in reparation for sin, and for the conversion of all to the Holy Catholic Church. I offer them for the intentions of our Holy Father the pope. Amen.

When we are ready for bed, we kneel by our beds. We think about how good God is. We tell God how much we love Him. We tell Him we are sorry for any bad things we have done this day. We make a good Act of Contrition. We promise God to try harder. We ask our guardian angel to help us. We say our Guardian Angel prayer.

Can you name some other times we pray during the day? We say the Rosary together with our family. We say the blessing before meals. We give thanks after meals. We say the Angelus at noon and at 6:00 in the evening. If we are up early, then we can also join the many others in praying the Angelus at 6:00 in the morning. We should pray throughout the day as we do our studies and our household chores.

1. St. Paul teaches us to "_____ _____."

2. If we say a _____ _____,
   then every action of our day becomes a prayer.

3. Name some other prayers we say during the day: _____

_____

Before we begin our prayers, we make the Sign of the Cross. We fold our hands and we bow our heads and begin to pray.

Once Jesus was sitting on a hillside teaching His Apostles. They said to Him, "Lord, teach us how to pray." Jesus taught them the Our Father. That is why it is also called "The Lord's Prayer." The Our Father comes right from Jesus Himself, and so it is called the perfect prayer.

Our Father, Who art in Heaven, (We pray to God our Father in Heaven.)

hallowed be Thy Name. (God's Name is holy. Hallowed means holy.)

Thy kingdom come. (We are asking God to let all people on Earth know about His heavenly kingdom.)

Thy will be done on earth as it is in Heaven. (We must do God's Will the way the saints do in Heaven.)

Give us this day our daily bread, (We ask God to provide food for our bodies, but especially ask Him to give us Holy Communion, the food for our souls.)

and forgive us our trespasses (We beg forgiveness for our sins.)

as we forgive those who trespass against us; (We forgive all those who have hurt us.)

and lead us not into temptation (We ask God to keep us away from sin and all the things which may cause us to sin.)

but deliver us from evil. (We ask God to save us from all danger and from all sin.)

Amen. (So be it.)

Lord, teach me to pray!

1. The Our Father was given to us by _____.

2. Another name for the Our Father is the _____

   _____.

3. Because no mere man gave us this prayer but God Himself, it is

   called the _____ prayer.

The Holy Sacrifice of the Mass is the greatest prayer of all. When we go into the church, we dip our fingers into the holy water and make the Sign of the Cross. We genuflect to Our Lord in the tabernacle before entering the pew. We kneel on the kneeler and pray before we sit. A Catholic church is the most holy place on Earth. We must show God reverence when we are there. We do so by behaving in the proper way. We must not talk, laugh, or giggle in church. If there is a noise, we should not be curious in turning our heads to see what has happened. We should be sure to get to church and in our pew before the Mass begins. When it is time to kneel, stand, or sit, we should do so reverently as perfect little Christian ladies and gentlemen. We should sit straight. Silently, we think about God and pray. We hear Him best when there is silence.

At the Holy Sacrifice of the Mass, we say all four types of prayer:

We adore God: "Glory to God in the Highest and peace to men of good will."

We thank God: "Let us give thanks to the Lord our God. It is right and just."

We tell God we are sorry for our sins: "Lord, have mercy on us."

We ask God for special favors: "O Lord, I am not worthy that You should enter under my roof, but only say the word, and my soul shall be healed."

We are attentive to all the prayers of the Mass. We ask for the graces of the final blessing and sing the closing hymn. We remain standing until the priest leaves the sanctuary and the hymn is finished. We should not be in a hurry to leave church, but should kneel in further adoration of Our Lord. We ought to ask Him for His help during the coming day or week. When Mass is over, we do not talk to our friends until we are outside the church. In these ways, we show Jesus just how reverent we can be and that we love being with Him.

Praise and adoration ever more be given to the Holy Sacrament of the Altar.

1. A _____ _____ is the most holy place on Earth.

2. On entering church, we dip our fingers into the _____ _____, then bless ourselves with the Sign of the Cross.

3. We _____ before entering the pew.

Questions for Week Thirty

Day 1

1. What is prayer?

   Prayer is the lifting of our mind and heart to God. Prayer is talking to God.

2. What are the four types of prayer?

   The four types of prayer are:

   1) adoration,
   2) thanksgiving,
   3) reparation,
   4) petition.

Day 2

1. How often should we pray?

   The Bible tells us we ought to pray always. Everything we do can be a prayer.

2. How can our whole day be a prayer?

   Our whole day can be a prayer if we begin the day by saying a Morning Offering.

3. What prayer tells God we are sorry for our sins?

   The Act of Contrition tells God we are sorry for our sins.

Day 3

1. How should we start each prayer?

   We should start each prayer with the Sign of the Cross.

2. What prayer is the perfect prayer?

   The Lord's Prayer, the Our Father, is the perfect prayer because it was given to us by Jesus Himself.

Day 4

At the Holy Sacrifice of the Mass, we

1. _____ God;

2. _____ God;

3. tell God we are _____ for our sins; and

4. we _____ God for special favors.

The Apostles' Creed

Do you know how to pray the Apostles' Creed? It begins: "I believe in God, the Father Almighty...". The Apostles' Creed is an act of Faith because we say, "I believe." We believe in all that the Apostles have taught us. We believe in all that the Catholic Church teaches because it was founded or begun by Our Lord Jesus Christ. Jesus has told us it is true. We have learned everything in the Apostles' Creed this school year. This week, we will go through the Apostles' Creed line by line. In this way, we can better understand things we need to know and believe in order to get to Heaven.

I believe in God, the Father Almighty, We believe that God the Father is almighty. He can do anything.

Creator of Heaven and Earth. He made Heaven, the stars, Earth, man, and all of creation.

And in Jesus Christ, His only Son, Our Lord. We believe that Jesus is God's Son. Jesus is God. Jesus is our dear Lord.

Who was conceived by the Holy Spirit, The third Person of the Blessed Trinity, the Holy Spirit, placed the Son of God into the womb of Mary, His Mother.

born of the Virgin Mary. Jesus was born on Christmas Day to His most pure Mother Mary.

Holy Trinity, one God, have mercy on us.

1. The Apostles' Creed is an act of _____.

2. In this prayer, we believe all that was taught to us by the

   _____.

3. The Catholic Church was started by _____ _____.

He suffered under Pontius Pilate. The Roman leader Pontius Pilate condemned Jesus to death.

was crucified, died, and was buried. Jesus died on the Cross and was buried in the tomb.

He descended into Hell. By dying on the Cross, Jesus opened the gates of Heaven. While His Body lay in the tomb, His Soul descended to a place where the souls of good people had been waiting for Him. Jesus took them to Heaven. The gates of Heaven were opened at last! This place was not the Hell where the devil lives. It was a place where all good men waited until the gates of Heaven were opened. We call this place the Limbo of the Fathers. These people were happy because they knew they would see God when Our Lord Jesus would open the gates of Heaven.

The third day He rose again from the dead. Jesus rose from the dead on Easter Sunday. This proved that He is God!

Mary, Queen of Apostles, keep us faithful to the Church.

1. Jesus suffered under _____ _____.

2. Jesus was _____, died, and was buried.

3. On the third day, Jesus _____ from the dead.

He ascended into Heaven, Jesus stayed on Earth for forty days after He rose from the dead. He then ascended or rose into Heaven by His own Divine Power. We celebrate His Ascension forty days after Easter. It is a holy day of obligation. Do you remember which Mystery of the Rosary the Ascension is? It is the Second Glorious Mystery.

and sitteth at the right hand of God, the Father Almighty. In Heaven, Jesus' throne is at the right hand of God the Father.

From thence He shall come to judge the living and the dead. Everyone who dies stands before Jesus at the Particular Judgment which takes place right after our death, and again at the Last Judgment at the end of the world.

Praised and blessed forever be the Holy Name of Jesus.

1. Jesus ascended into _____ by His own Divine Power.

2. In Heaven, Jesus sits at the _____ _____ of God the Father.

3. Jesus will judge us twice: at the _____

    Judgment and at the _____ Judgment.

I believe in the Holy Spirit, The Holy Spirit is God, the Third Person of the Blessed Trinity.

the Holy Catholic Church, God's one true Church is the Catholic Church.

the communion of saints, The saints in Heaven, the faithful on Earth, and the holy souls in Purgatory join together with Christ as our Head to form the Catholic Church.

the forgiveness of sins, By the Sacrament of Penance, Jesus forgives our sins if we are truly sorry.

the resurrection of the body, At the end of the world, Jesus will come again for the Last Judgment. Our bodies will rise and be united to our souls once again.

and life everlasting. Amen. Oh, how we long to live with God forever! God made us to   know, love, and serve Him in this world in order that we may be happy with Him forever in Heaven. "Amen" means that I truly believe everything that I have said and that it is true.

Holy Spirit, enlighten my mind and strengthen my will to do good and avoid evil.

1. The Holy Spirit is God the _____ _____ of the Blessed Trinity.

2. God's true Church is the _____ _____.

3. In the communion of saints are the _____ in Heaven, the _____ on Earth, and the _____ souls in Purgatory.

177

Questions for Week Thirty-one

Day 1

1. What are contained in the Apostles' Creed?

   In the Apostles' Creed are contained the chief truths of the Catholic Faith.

2. Why is it called the Apostles' Creed?

   It is called the Apostles' Creed because it was given to us directly from the Apostles.

Day 2

Where did Our Lord descend after His death?

When we say, "He descended into Hell," we do not mean the Hell of the damned. Our Lord descended to a place where all the just souls had been waiting since the time of Adam.

Day 3

1. How many times will we be judged?

   We will be judged two times: alone at the Particular Judgment immediately after our body dies, and together with everyone else who has ever lived at the Last Judgment at the end of the world.

2. Who will be our Judge?

   Jesus Christ, Who died for us, will be our Judge.

More on the Commandments

The Fourth Commandment

We learned about the Ten Commandments earlier in this book, but only briefly. Some Commandments are very important for children to study and remember. So this week, we will study the Fourth Commandment.

The Fourth Commandment of God is: "Honor thy father and thy mother."

The first three Commandments of God tell us about our obligation to God. The First Commandment is: "I am the Lord thy God. Thou shalt not have strange gods before Me." In this First Commandment, God is commanding that He be loved, respected, and honored above everyone and everything else.

The last seven Commandments tell us about our duties to our family, friends, and neighbors. Like the First Commandment above, the first Commandment in this group tells us we must love, respect, and obey our parents: "Honor thy father and thy mother."

We owe supreme respect and honor to God because He gave us life. We owe the highest human love, respect, and honor to our parents who acted with God to give us life.

Immaculate Heart of Mary, deliver us from all dangers.

1. The Fourth Commandment of God is: "_____ thy father and thy mother."

2. We owe love and respect to our parents because they gave us

    _____.

179

"Honor thy father and thy mother."

We are commanded by the Fourth Commandment to honor our parents. This means that we must show them respect at all times. We are commanded to love our parents. We are commanded to obey our parents. We are commanded to help our parents if they are in need.

This means that if our parents ask us to set the table, we do it right away, even if we have not finished playing our game. This means that when Mother asks us to do a chore, we do not complain. This means that we always speak with respect to Dad and Mom even when we are upset. This means we sometimes help our little brother or sister when Mother is busy. This means that when we see Mom or Dad needing help, we rush to help even before we are asked.

The Fourth Commandment tells us to show our parents our love by not arguing with them. Our parents are given special graces by God in the Sacrament of Matrimony to know what is best for their children. God gives parents special rights and duties to take care of their children both physically, such as by providing a home, and spiritually, such as by teaching them about the Catholic Faith.

We understand that God made us and put us in this family with our parents who will show us how to be good so we can go to Heaven.

God chose the best parents for us. We need to thank God for giving us our parents by being kind and obedient and loving.

Immaculate Heart of Mary, make our family life holy.

1. We need to thank God for giving us our _____.

2. When we are asked to do a chore, we do not _____.

3. We are commanded to _____ our parents when they are in need.

"Honor thy father and thy mother."

The Fourth Commandment forbids disrespect, unkindness, and disobedience to our parents.

There are four things we are commanded by the Fourth Commandment. We are commanded to respect our parents, love our parents, obey our parents, and help our parents. Our parents take the place of God on Earth. They are the authority we must respect, love, obey, and help. God gave our parents authority over us so that they will show us how to behave and teach us about obeying God's Laws. Parents are home schooling because they believe they can better train and teach their children according to the truths of Our Lord Jesus Christ.

Catholic parents are trying to be obedient to God's Law. If we are disobedient to our parents, we are disobedient to God as well since He planned for us to be obedient the parents He gave us. We should always answer our parents respectfully. We should speak to our parents in a proper tone of voice. If we do not, then we commit a sin which should be told in Confession. We should tell Jesus we are sorry is we are disrespectful or disobedient to our parents, and then we should tell our parents we are sorry.

We should be obedient about our chores. We should do what we are told, and we should do it the first time we are told. We should do it in the best way we can. If we do not, then we commit a sin of disobedience to our parents which should be told in Confession. We should do our studies diligently. If not, then we commit a sin of disobedience to our parents which should be told in Confession. We should always remember to say, "I'm sorry."

Of the last seven Commandments, the most important one for children is this: "Honor thy father and thy mother."

Immaculate Heart of Mary, help those who are dear to us.

The Fourth Commandment forbids _____,

_____, and _____ to our parents.

"Honor thy father and thy mother."

In the first three Commandments, God gave us Laws to show our duty to Him. The Fourth Commandment is the most important in our duties to others: "Honor thy father and thy mother."

In the Fourth Commandment, God shows us what our duty to our parents is. We should respect our parents. We should love our parents. We should obey our parents. We should help our parents. We should pray for our parents. We should do special things for them to show we love them.

Jesus showed how much He loved His Mother when they were at the wedding feast at Cana. Jesus changed water into wine for Mary, even though she never explicitly asked Him. He simply did what she wished. When we love, we do things because it will please the other person. We should show our love for our parents by doing things that will please them.

Jesus loves Mary and Joseph so much that, even though He is God, He obeyed them. When they asked Him to come home with them from the Temple, He went immediately with them to their home in Nazareth.

When Jesus was praying to God the Father, and was thinking about His suffering and death on the Cross, He said to God His Father: "Not My Will, but Thine be done."

You can always tell when someone really loves another person. He always shows respect and kindness, and always helps, even before being asked.

Let's follow Jesus by always doing just what we are told to do, right away.

Let's follow Jesus by always helping, even before we are asked.

Jesus will be pleased because we are obeying one of the most important of all of His Ten Commandments: "Honor thy father and thy mother."

Immaculate Heart of Mary, pray for our dear country.

1. Jesus showed how much He loved His Mother when they were at

   the wedding feast at _____.

2. We show our love for our parents by doing things that will

   _____ them.

Questions for Week Thirty-two

Day 1

1. What is the Fourth Commandment of God?

   The Fourth Commandment of God is: "Honor thy father and thy mother."

2. About what are the first three Commandments of God?

   The first three Commandments are about our duty towards God.

3. About what are the next seven Commandments of God?

   The next seven Commandments of God are about our duty towards our family, friends, and neighbors.

Day 2

What are we commanded by the Fourth Commandment?

By the Fourth Commandment we are commanded to respect and love our parents, to obey them, and to help them when they are in need.

Day 3

1. What does the Fourth Commandment forbid?

   The Fourth Commandment forbids disrespect, unkindness, and disobedience to our parents.

2. Of the seven Commandments that relate to others, which one is the most important?

   Of the seven Commandments that relate to others, the Fourth Commandment is the most important.

Day 4

How do we show our love for our parents?

We show our love for our parents by respect and kindness, always obeying right away, and always helping, even before we are asked.

More on the Fifth Commandment

Another Commandment which is important for children is the Fifth Commandment: "Thou shalt not kill."

Some people think that they cannot break the Fifth Commandment because they are not going to kill anyone. However, the Fifth Commandment does not mean only that you should not kill anyone. The Fifth Commandment also means that you should not hurt anyone.

What are we commanded by the Fifth Commandment? By the Fifth Commandment we are commanded to take proper care of our souls and bodies, and also those of our neighbor. The Fifth Commandment forbids not only murder and suicide, but also quarreling, fighting, excessive or unjust anger, hatred, revenge, and bad example. Do you know why a bad example is a sin against the Fifth Commandment? A bad example teaches another to commit a sin. Sin can kill the life of grace in our souls.

God wants us to remember that we are all brothers and sisters in Jesus Christ. God is our Father in Heaven. He made everyone. Since He made us all, we are all brothers and sisters. God our Father does not want us to argue or fight. He does not want us to hate, or to set a bad example. We must be very careful of what we say and how we behave in front of our younger brothers and sisters. They will learn by our words and actions, and so these must be good examples for them.

Mother and Father love all their children, and it hurts them to see their children being unkind to one another. Mother and Father love all their children just as God loves all His children in the world.

We must be kind to one another. It is wrong to fight with others. We must love our neighbor as we love ourselves. If others are unkind to us, we must not be unkind to them. We must love and forgive them. We must pray for them, too.

"Love one another as I have loved you," said Jesus.

Heart of Jesus, full of goodness and love, have mercy on us.

1. The Fifth Commandment of God is: "Thou shalt not _____.

2. The Fifth Commandment also forbids quarreling, fighting, excessive or unjust anger, hatred, revenge, and bad

    _____.

"Thou shalt not kill."

The Fifth Commandment forbids us to quarrel. It especially forbids us to quarrel with our brothers and sisters. God has given us the people in our family. They are the most important persons in the world to us. We must love them, help them, pray for them, and be kind to them at all times.

The Fifth Commandment forbids excessive or violent arguing. It especially forbids excessive or violent arguement with our parents. It also forbids excessive or violent argument with our brothers and sisters, as well as with friends and neighbors.

The Fifth Commandment forbids wrongful or destructive anger. There may be times in our life when anger is a right response, for example, when an injustice is committed against another. The Fifth Commandment forbids us to let our anger control us. It forbids us to be unkind even to the persons who make us angry. It forbids us to do things in our anger that destroy or injure.

Hatred is a sin against the Fifth Commandment. Hatred is usually a serious sin. While we must hate sin, God commands us to love the person who sins by praying for him.

God commands us: "Love your neighbor as yourself." This means our parents, other family members, friends, and neighbors.

Jesus said, "Blessed are the peacemakers, for they shall be called children of God." If we keep the Fifth Commandment, our homes will be blessed with the peace of God.

Heart of Jesus, King and Center of all Hearts, have mercy on us.

1. The Fifth Commandment forbids us to _____ or

   _____ with our brothers and sisters.

2. "Blessed are the _____, for they shall be

   called _____ of God."

"Thou shalt not kill."

By the Fifth Commandment we are commanded to take proper care of our own spiritual and bodily welfare, and also that of our neighbor. The care we take of our souls is our spiritual welfare. The care we take of our bodies is our bodily welfare.

We take care of our spiritual welfare by saying our daily prayers, going to Confession regularly, and receiving Holy Communion reverently and frequently, once we have made our First Holy Communion.

We take care of our bodily welfare by taking care of our health, and obeying safety rules. We should cross the street at the light. We should not ride our bike in the road. We should eat the fruits and vegetables that Mother gives us. We should eat candy only when Mother gives us permission, and we must be careful not to eat so much that we get sick. When we do not do these things, we are breaking the Fifth Commandment.

We take care of the spiritual welfare of others by praying for them, including the holy souls in Purgatory, such as our grandparents and other relatives. We must be sure to give good example to others, especially our brothers and sisters.

We take care of the bodily welfare of others by not being careless when we play with them. Sometimes accidents happen because some children do not care about the welfare of others.

On the playground, we must be careful not to push the swings into the air so far that someone can get hit. We must never throw balls at other children, or trip anyone. On the slide, we must be careful and not go down too soon, or we may hurt the child in front of us. Good children know that these things are not part of play. Good children do not do hurtful things that are against the Fifth Commandment.

God, all powerful and good, have mercy on us.

1. We take care of our spiritual welfare by saying our daily

   _____.

2. We take care of the spiritual welfare of others by giving good

   _____.

"Thou shalt not kill."

The Fifth Commandment forbids murder and suicide, quarreling, fighting, unjust or excessive or violent anger, hatred, revenge, and bad example.

Revenge is doing something bad to someone because he did something bad to you.

Jesus said, "Do good to those who hate you; pray for those who persecute you." If our little brother breaks our toy, even if he did it on purpose, it is a sin to take revenge. Revenge is a very bad sin because it is doing evil to another person deliberately, on purpose.

Giving bad example is a sin against the Fifth Commandment. If you talk back to your mother and little sister is watching you, you have committed two sins: you have been disrespectful to your mother, and you have given bad example to your sister. You have shown your sister how to sin. Speaking or acting in a sinful way with another person looking on, is encouraging that person to commit the sin also. Bad example is a sin. Our Lord Jesus said that it would be better for an adult to drown in the sea than to give bad example to a child.

Bad example affects the spiritual welfare of the person who is watching the bad example. In the case of bad example, a person needs to repair the damage as far as possible. If you spoke disrespectfully to your mother in front of your little sister, you need to apologize to your mother in front of your little sister.

We must be careful never to break the Fifth Commandment.

Holy Virgin, full of grace, pray for us.

1. Jesus said, "Do good to those who _____ you."

2. _____ is doing something bad to someone because he did something bad to you.

3. In the case of bad example, you must _____ the damage as far as possible.

Questions for Week Thirty-three

Day 1

* 1. What is the Fifth Commandment of God?

   The Fifth Commandment of God is: "Thou shalt not kill."

* 2. What are we commanded by the Fifth Commandment?

   By the Fifth Commandment, we are commanded to take proper care of our own spiritual and bodily well-being and that of our neighbor.

Day 2

1. What does the Fifth Commandment forbid?

   The Fifth Commandment forbids murder and suicide, and also fighting, excessive or violent or unjust anger, hatred, revenge, and bad example.

2. Why is bad example a sin against the Fifth Commandment?

   Bad example is a sin against the Fifth Commandment because it teaches another person to commit a sin, thus hurting or, in the case of mortal sin, killing the life of grace in the soul.

Day 3

1. How do we take care of our spiritual welfare?

   We take care of our spiritual welfare by saying our daily prayers, going to Confession regularly, and receiving Holy Communion reverently and frequently, if we have made our First Holy Communion.

2. How do we take care of the spiritual welfare of others?

   We take care of the spiritual welfare of others by praying for them and by giving good example.

Day 4

1. Why is revenge a very bad sin?

   Revenge is a very bad sin because it is doing evil to another person on purpose.

2. If a person has given bad example, what should he do?

   A person should repair the damage as much as possible and, in the future, work to be a good example.

More on the Eighth Commandment

Another important commandment for children to remember is the Eighth Commandment of God: "Thou shalt not bear false witness against thy neighbor."

"To bear false witness" means to lie about our neighbor. We remember that everyone is our neighbor. We must never lie. The Eighth Commandment commands us to tell the truth in all things. The Eighth Commandment forbids lying.

Lying is a sin. How can we be trusted if we lie?

Our Lord Jesus said the devil is the father of all lies.

Lying can be a serious sin in serious matters. Lying can harm a person, a family, a parish, a town, or a whole country. A person who lies cannot be trusted. Once others lose their trust in someone, it is very difficult to gain it back. To knowingly say what is untrue is to tell a lie. It is a sin against the Eighth Commandment of God.

Mary, Our Lady of Victory, pray for us.

1. The Eighth Commandment of God is: "Thou shalt not bear

   _____ witness against thy neighbor."

2. The Eighth Commandment forbids _____.

3. By the Eighth Commandment we are commanded to tell the

   _____ in all things.

"Thou shalt not bear false witness against thy neighbor."

The Eighth Commandment means that we must never tell a lie against our neighbor. The Eighth Commandment commands us to be truthful in all things.

Lies offend God. In the Bible, Our Lord Jesus tells us that He is the Way, the Truth, and the Life. We are never permitted to tell a lie.

Sometimes children are tempted to lie if they have done something that might get them into trouble. We must always do the right thing. We must pray to our guardian angel to help us speak truthfully, especially when it is hard to do so. Remember that God will always give us the grace to do what is right. He will reward us with more graces when we are truthful. It is always wrong to lie.

If you tell a lie, you should repair the damage. If you have lied to others, you should go back to each person and tell the truth.

Mary, Mediatrix of all graces, pray for us.

1. Lies offend _____.

2. Jesus said "I am the Way, the _____, and the _____."

3. If you tell a lie, you should go back to the person and tell the _____.

"Thou shalt not bear false witness against thy neighbor."

The Eighth Commandment commands us to tell the truth in all things.

God gave us our tongues to speak the truth. It is against the Law of God to lie. God gave us our tongue to glorify Him, and to receive Jesus Himself in Holy Communion.

Do you remember the story of Joseph in the Old Testament? Because they were jealous of him, Joseph's brothers sold him to the Egyptians as a slave. The brothers lied to their father, and told him that Joseph was dead. God punished the wicked brothers and their families by sending a great famine into the land.

In the Bible, St. Paul wrote: "Put away lying, and speak truth each one with his neighbor." One time long ago, two mothers each had a baby. The first mother's baby died. She was so unhappy, that while the other mother slept, she stole her baby. The second mother went to King Solomon and said, "This woman has stolen my baby." The first mother lied and said, "No, it is my baby."

Now King Solomon was very wise. He was often called Wise King Solomon. He said to both women, "I will cut the baby in half, and then each of you can have half." The true mother screamed out in horror. "Oh, no!" she cried, "let that woman keep my baby. I want my baby to live!"

That is how Wise King Solomon found out who was the lying woman!

There have been many times when lying has caused bad things to happen.

NEVER TELL A LIE!

Our Lady of Lourdes, pray for us.

1. God gave us our _____ to speak the truth.

2. St. _____ wrote: "Put away lying, and speak truth."

3. Wise King _____ found out who was telling the truth.

"Thou shalt not bear false witness against thy neighbor."

The Eighth Commandment commands us always to speak the truth.

The first president of the United States was known for his great honesty. When he was a child, he chopped down his father's favorite cherry tree. When his father asked who chopped down the tree, George Washington bravely admitted it by saying, "Father, I cannot tell a lie. I chopped down your cherry tree, and I am sorry."

When George Washington grew up, people trusted him because he always told the truth. The people elected George Washington our first president because they knew he would always tell the truth.

When Mother asks who spilled the milk, we might be tempted to blame our little baby sister who cannot defend herself. When we tell a lie, we commit a sin against the Law of God, the Eighth Commandment.

Even though it may seem an unimportant little thing, no sin is a little thing. Each sin offends God. Sin is ugly to God, though He always loves us no matter what. Lies often offend others. A lie can cause harm to someone else as well as to ourselves. Many wise people have said that big criminals start out by committing little sins when they are young.

A virtue is a good habit. Let us practice good habits when we are children so that we will live virtuous lives when we are grown up.

Our Lady of Fatima, pray for us.

1. _____ _____ told the truth to his father about cutting down the cherry tree.

2. A _____ is a good habit.

3. Sin is _____ to God, though He continues to love us.

Questions for Week Thirty-four

Day 1

* 1. What is the Eighth Commandment of God?

The Eighth Commandment of God is, "Thou shalt not bear false witness against thy neighbor."

* 2. What are we commanded by the Eighth Commandment of God?

By the Eighth Commandment of God we are commanded to speak the truth in all things.

Day 2

1. Are we ever permitted to tell a lie?

No, we are never permitted to tell a lie.

2. What must we do if we tell a lie?

If we tell someone a lie, we should try to repair the damage.

Day 3

1. What can happen as a result of lying?

Lying can cause bad things to happen.

2. Tell the Old Testament story of Wise King Solomon and the lying mother.

Day 4

1. Why is no sin ever a little thing?

No sin is ever a little thing because each sin offends God. Sin is ugly to God.

2. Tell the story of little George Washington and the cherry tree.

Why Did God Make Us?

God made us because He loves us. He gave us life in order that we may know Him, love Him, and serve Him in this world. If we do, when we die He will take us to Heaven to share eternal happiness with Him and all the angels and saints. God made us so that we can know, love, and serve Him.

To know God, we must learn about Him. Everything we learn each day helps us to know God better. Every subject that we study, such as English, arithmetic, or science, helps us to know more about God. When we learn to read, we can read about God. When we learn science, we learn about the wonderful world God created. When we study arithmetic, we can learn about the order God has placed in His creation. Everything we learn, we learn for God.

We can never learn everything about God, but the more we know, the better we can love and serve Him. God wants us to spend our entire lives striving to know more and more about His work in order that we can become closer and closer to Him. That is why He made us. The more we know about God, the better we will want to serve Him. The more we know about God, the more we can see how glorious He is and just how much of us He deserves. He deserves all of us.

All through Thee, with Thee, and in Thee, O my God!

1. God made us because He _____ us.

2. In order to be with God in Heaven, we must _____,

   _____, and _____ Him in this world.

3. To know God, we must _____ about Him.

God wants us to show our love for Him in many ways. We must love Him with our whole heart and our whole soul. We must love Him with our whole mind and our whole strength. Every part of us must love God completely and without reserve. We must never hold any part of us back in our love of God. We must never make anything more important than God. God made us, and so we must love Him above all things. If we do not, we will not be happy with Him in Heaven.

Each time we are tempted to sin, we must stop and think, "What do I love?" "Whom do I love?" When temptation comes, quickly whisper a silent prayer to Jesus and say, "Help me, Jesus. I belong to You, Jesus. Help me to love You more because I want to be happy with You forever in Heaven."

I believe in Thee, I hope in Thee, I love Thee, I adore Thee, O Blessed Trinity!

1. We must love God with our whole _____, _____, _____, and _____.

2. We must love God _____ and without reserve.

3. God made us, and so we must love Him _____ all things.

The Laws of the Church

If we truly love God, then we want to serve Him. Our Lord Jesus came to Earth to teach us how to serve Him, His Father, and the Holy Spirit. Jesus told us to belong to His Holy Catholic Church. Jesus told His followers what we must do to serve God. Jesus started the Roman Catholic Church and made St. Peter the first pope. He made the Apostles the first bishops of His Church. He gave them powers to teach us, to rule us, and to sanctify us. There are six laws, or precepts, of the Church that every Catholic must follow. They are:

1. To assist at Mass on all Sundays and holy days of obligation.
2. To fast and abstain on the days appointed.
3. To confess our sins at least once a year.
4. To receive Holy Communion during the Easter time.
5. To contribute to the support of the Church.
6. To observe the laws of the Church concerning marriage.

O Jesus our Savior, assist Thy holy Church.

1. Jesus told us to belong to the _____ Church.

2. The Apostles were the first _____ of the Catholic Church.

3. Our Lord gave the Apostles powers to _____ us, to _____ us, and to _____ us.

The Heart of the Commandments

Our Lord Jesus teaches us in the Bible: "If you love Me, you will keep My Commandments." We have already studied the Ten Commandments. Let us carefully follow them in our daily life.

Jesus tells us about two other commandments in the Gospels. When the disciples ask Him, He says the two most important commandments are:

1. "Thou shalt love the Lord thy God with thy whole heart, and with thy whole soul, and with thy whole mind, and with thy whole strength.

2. Thou shalt love thy neighbor as thyself."

Jesus tells us all the Ten Commandments are contained in these. If we love God, we will gladly obey His first three Commandments. If we truly love our neighbor, we will obey the next seven Commandments. If we do not love our neighbor, we cannot love God.

From this we learn that love is the most important Commandment of God. The Ten Commandments and the laws of His Church help us to love and serve God. They help us by telling us **how** to love God and one another.

Oh my God, I love Thee above all things,
I love my neighbor as myself for love of Thee.

1. All Ten Commandments can be summed up into _____ commandments.

2. The Ten Commandments help us to _____ and _____ God.

Questions for Week Thirty-five

Day 1

* 1. Why did God make us?

    God made us to show forth His goodness and to make us happy with Him in Heaven.

* 2. What must we do to be happy with God in Heaven?

    To be happy with God in Heaven we must know, love, and serve God in this world.

Day 2

1. How should we love God?

    We should love God with our whole heart, soul, mind, and strength. We must love God above all things.

* 2. From whom do we learn to know, love and serve God?

    We learn to know, love, and serve God from Jesus Christ, the Son of God, Who teaches us through the Catholic Church.

Day 3

1. What power did Jesus give the Apostles and His Church?

    Jesus gave the Apostles and His Church the power to teach, rule, and sanctify.

2. How many laws of the Church are there?

    There are six laws or precepts of the Catholic Church.

Day 4

What are the two Great Commandments given to us by Jesus?

The two Great Commandments given to us by Jesus are:

1. "Thou shalt love the Lord thy God with thy whole heart, and with thy whole soul, and with thy whole mind, and with thy whole strength.

2. Thou shalt love thy neighbor as thyself."

Fourth Quarter Review

WEEK THIRTY-SIX: Day 1   Review work from Weeks 28 and 29

WEEK THIRTY-SIX: Day 2   Review work from Weeks 30, 31, and 32

WEEK THIRTY-SIX: Day 3   Review work from Weeks 33, 34, and 35

WEEK THIRTY-SIX: Day 4   Take Fourth Quarter Test

Note: If extra time is needed for review, use Day 4 to review. Use Day 5 to take the test.

Stained Glass Index

Religion 3 for Young Catholics

ANSWER KEY

Week One: Day 1
1. everything
2. whole
3. happy

Week One: Day 2
1. died
2. perfect
3. above
4. neighbor

Week One: Day 3
1. children
2. listen
3. talk

Week One: Day 4
1. Morning Offering
2. love

Week Two: Day 1
1. knows
2. always
3. Supreme Being

Week Two: Day 2
1. was
2. die
3. everything
4. good
5. tabernacle

Week Two: Day 3
1. Blessed Trinity
2. mystery
3. Cross

Week Three: Day 1
1. nothing
2. spirits
3. messengers

Week Three: Day 2
1. angels
2. free
3. Michael
4. Lucifer

Week Three: Day 3
1. rewarded
2. guardian angel
3. messengers

Week Three: Day 4
1. sin
2. forever
3. guardian

Week Four: Day 1
1. body; soul
2. image; likeness
3. sickness; death

Week Four: Day 2
1. Knowledge; Good; Evil
2. tested

Week Four: Day 3
1. serpent
2. friendship
3. grace

Week Four: Day 4
1. Original Sin
2. Savior
3. Baptism

Week Five: Day 1
1. Cain; Abel
2. Abel
3. Cain

Week Five: Day 2
1. killed
2. actual
3. wander

Week Five: Day 3
1. thought; desire; word; action; omission
2. omission

Week Five: Day 4
1. mortal; venial
2. enemy
3. less

Week Six: Day 1
1. Moses
2. Ten Commandments

Week Six: Day 2
1. holy
2. covenant
3. Commandments

Week Six: Day 3
1. false
2. True
3. strange gods

Week Six: Day 4
1. heads
2. name

Week Seven: Day 1
1. Sunday
2. work
3. body

Week Seven: Day 2
1. obey, honor, respect
2. respect
3. religious

Week Seven: Day 3
1. forgive
2. evil
3. Fifth

Week Seven: Day 4
1. clean, pure
2. Blessed Mother
3. Mary

Week Eight: Day 1
1. steal
2. return
3. damage

Week Eight: Day 2
1. false witness
2. lie
3. bad

Week Eight: Day 3
1. thoughts
2. satisfied
3. covet

Week Ten: Day 1
1. Savior
2. Man
3. Will
4. Advent

Week Ten: Day 2
1. Blessed Virgin Mary
2. sin
3. grace

Week Ten: Day 3
1. Gabriel
2. message
3. offended

Week Ten: Day 4
1. Annunciation
2. Visitation
3. John

Week Eleven: Day 1
1. foster-father
2. carpenter
3. Bethlehem

Week Eleven: Day 2
1. inns
2. shepherds
3. manger

Week Eleven: Day 3
1. Christmas
2. December 25
3. family

Week Eleven: Day 4
1. star
2. gold; frankincense; myrrh
3. tabernacle

Week Twelve: Day 1
1. disappeared
2. kill
3. angel

Week Twelve: Day 2
1. dream
2. Egypt
3. Holy Innocents

Week Twelve: Day 3
1. carpenter
2. helped
3. follow

Week Twelve: Day 4
1. King Herod
2. Nazareth

Week Thirteen: Day 1
1. Jerusalem
2. three
3. teaching

Week Thirteen: Day 2
1. Jesus; Mary
2. baptized
3. Blessed Trinity

Week Thirteen: Day 3
1. fast; pray
2. one; sent
3. St. Peter

Week Thirteen: Day 4
1. children
2. Our Father
3. perfect

Week Fourteen: Day 1
1. miracle
2. wedding
3. Mother

Week Fourteen: Day 2
1. loaves; fishes
2. twelve
3. miracles

Week Fourteen: Day 3
1. storm
2. water
3. everything

Week Fourteen: Day 4
1. Lazarus
2. 4 days
3. Martha

Week Fifteen: Day 1
1. Jairus
2. faith
3. Mass

Week Fifteen: Day 2
1. Pharisees
2. Savior
3. blindness

Week Fifteen: Day 3
1. parables
2. neighbor

Week Fifteen: Day 4
1. God
2. remember
3. Bible

Week Sixteen: Day 1
1. suffering; death
2. self-denial or sacrifice

Week Sixteen: Day 2
1. three
2. Holy Thursday
3. Holy Eucharist (or Blessed
   Sacrament)

Week Sixteen: Day 3
1. pray
2. asleep
3. kiss

Week Sixteen: Day 4
1. Pontius Pilate
2. innocent
3. washed

Week Seventeen: Day 1
1. Cross

Week Seventeen: Day 4
1. fourteen
2. Lent

Week Nineteen: Day 1
1. stole
2. Peter; John
3. wounds

Week Nineteen: Day 2
1. risen
2. glorified
3. reunited

Week Nineteen: Day 3
1. forty
2. Catholic
3. pope

Week Nineteen: Day 4
1. all nations
2. forty

Week Twenty: Day 1
1. pray
2. alone
3. Third Person

Week Twenty: Day 2
1. nine
2. fire
3. soldiers

Week Twenty: Day 3
1. Pentecost
2. languages
3. Upper Room

Week Twenty: Day 4
1. birthday
2. beginning
3. guides

Week Twenty-one: Day 1
1. Heaven
2. bishops; priests
3. grace

Week Twenty-one: Day 2
1. seven
2. sacraments
3. bishops; priests

Week Twenty-one: Day 3
1. Baptism
2. Holy Spirit
3. Original Sin

Week Twenty-one: Day 4
1. Holy Spirit
2. sin

Week Twenty-two: Day 1
1. Penance
2. forgive
3. forgive; forgiven

Week Twenty-two: Day 2
1. mortal; venial
2. destroys
3. Confession

Week Twenty-two: Day 3
1. five
2. examine
3. Ten Commandments

Week Twenty-two: Day 4
1. confessional
2. Jesus
3. Act; Contrition

Week Twenty-three: Day 1
Body; Blood

Week Twenty-three: Day 2
1. Jesus Christ
2. Blood

Week Twenty-three: Day 3
1. mortal sin
2. one hour
3. Act; Contrition

Week Twenty-three: Day 4
1. thank
2. love
3. help
4. pray

Week Twenty-four: Day 1
1. Confirmation
2. bishop
3. soldiers; Christ

Week Twenty-four: Day 2
1. men; priests
2. man
3. saint

Week Twenty-four: Day 3
1. Matrimony
2. Holy Family
3. know; love; serve

Week Twenty-four: Day 4,
1. Anointing of the Sick
2. strength
3. health

Week Twenty-five: Day 1
1. Mass
2. Consecration
3. spirits

Week Twenty-five: Day 2
1. Sacrifice
2. unbloody
3. priest

Week Twenty-five: Day 3
1. Cross
2. bloody
3. unbloody

Week Twenty-five: Day 4
1. Jesus

Week Twenty-six: Day 1
1. sins
2. Sacrifice
3. easy

Week Twenty-six: Day 2
1. Purgatory
2. Heaven; Purgatory; Earth

Week Twenty-six: Day 3
1. Catholic Church
2. pope

Week Twenty-six: Day 4
1. prevail
2. true
3. pope (or Holy Father)
4. Jesus

Week Twenty-eight: Day 1
1. Mother
2. St. Dominic

Week Twenty-eight: Day 2
1. Gabriel
2. Savior
3. teaching

Week Twenty-eight: Day 4
1. sweat
2. people
3. forgive

Week Twenty-nine: Day 1
1. six
2. Sundays
3. January 1

Week Twenty-nine: Day 2
1. Ascension
2. Assumption
3. Mass

Week Twenty-nine: Day 3
1. November 1
2. saint
3. saints

Week Twenty-nine: Day 4
1. Immaculate Conception
2. December 8
3. Christmas

Week Thirty: Day 1
1. minds; hearts
2. four
3. adore

Week Thirty: Day 2
1. pray always
2. Morning Offering
3. Guardian Angel prayer, Angelus, Act of Contrition, the Rosary, blessing before and after meals

Week Thirty: Day 3
1. Jesus
2. Lord's Prayer
3. perfect

Week Thirty: Day 4
1. Catholic church
2. holy water
3. genuflect

Week Thirty-one: Day 1
1. faith
2. Apostles
3. Jesus Christ

Week Thirty-one: Day 2
1. Pontius Pilate
2. crucified
3. rose

Week Thirty-one: Day 3
1. Heaven
2. right hand
3. Particular, Last

Week Thirty-one: Day 4
1. Third Person
2. Catholic Church
3. saints; faithful; holy

Week Thirty-two: Day 1
1. Honor
2. life

Week Thirty-two: Day 2
1. parents
2. complain
3. help

Week Thirty-two: Day 3
disrespect; unkindness; disobedience

Week Thirty-two: Day 4
1. Cana
2. please

Week Thirty-three: Day 1
1. kill
2. example

Week Thirty-three: Day 2
1. quarrel; argue
2. peacemakers; children

Week Thirty-three: Day 3
1. prayers
2. example

Week Thirty-three: Day 4
1. hate
2. Revenge
3. repair

Week Thirty-four: Day 1
1. false
2. lying
3. truth

Week Thirty-four: Day 2
1. God
2. Truth; Life
3. truth

Week Thirty-four: Day 3
1. tongues
2. Paul
3. Solomon

Week Thirty-four: Day 4
1. George Washington
2. virtue
3. ugly

Week Thirty-five: Day 1
1. loves
2. know; love; serve
3. learn

Week Thirty-five: Day 2
1. heart; soul; mind; strength
2. completely
3. above

Week Thirty-five: Day 3
1. Catholic
2. bishops
3. teach; rule; sanctify

Week Thirty-five: Day 4
1. two
2. love; serve